Problem Regions of Europe
General Editor: **D. I. Scargill**

Saar-Lorraine

David Burtenshaw

Oxford University Press 1976

Oxford University Press, Ely House, London W.1

OXFORD LONDON GLASGOW NEW YORK
TORONTO MELBOURNE WELLINGTON CAPE TOWN
IBADAN NAIROBI DAR ES SALAAM LUSAKA ADDIS ABABA
KUALA LUMPUR SINGAPORE JAKARTA HONG KONG TOKYO
DELHI BOMBAY CALCUTTA MADRAS KARACHI

© Oxford University Press 1976

I would like to record my thanks to the many
government officers, industrial concerns,
individuals, and friends who have helped in
the preparation of this book. The maps were
drawn by Sarah Hancock and Jack Render of
the Cartographic Unit, Portsmouth Polytechnic.
I also wish to thank Portsmouth Polytechnic
for their financial support for fieldwork.
D.B.

Filmset by BAS Printers Limited, Wallop, Hampshire
and printed in Great Britain
at the University Press, Oxford
by Vivian Ridler, Printer to the University

Editor's Preface

Great economic and social changes have taken place in Europe in recent years. The agricultural workforce in the west was halved, for example, during the 1950s and 1960s. This unprecedented flight from the land has made possible some much-needed reorganization of farm holdings but it has also created problems, not least that of finding uses for land in the highlands and elsewhere where it is no longer profitable to farm. Closely related is the difficulty of maintaining services to a much diminished rural population or of providing new kinds of services for the holidaymakers who increasingly buy up rural properties.

Contraction of the labour force has also taken place in many traditional industries. The coal-mining industry alone has shed two-thirds of its workforce since 1950. The resulting problems have been especially serious in those mining or manufacturing districts which have a high level of dependence on a single source of employment—a not uncommon result of Europe's industrial past—and the efforts of those who seek to attract new industries are often thwarted by a legacy of pollution, bad housing, and soured labour relations.

Quite a different set of problems has arisen in the great cities of Europe such as London and Paris and in the conurbations of closely linked cities well exemplified by Randstad Holland. Here are problems due to growth brought about by the expansion of consumer-orientated manufacturing and still more by the massive increase in office jobs which proliferate in 'down-town' business districts. The problems are economic, social and political, and they include the effects of congestion, of soaring land values, of the increasing divorce of place of residence from place of work, and of the difficulty of planning a metropolitan region that may be shared between many independent-minded local authorities.

The problems resulting from change are not passing ones; indeed they exhibit a persistence that amply justifies their study on an areal basis. Hence the *Problem Regions of Europe* series. The volumes in the series have all been written by geographers who, by the nature of their discipline, can take a broadly based approach to description and analysis. Geographers in the past have been reluctant to base their studies on problem regions since the problem was often of a temporary nature, less enduring than the 'personality' of the region but the magnitude of present-day problems has even resulted in the suggestion that regions should be defined in terms of the problems that confront them.

Certain themes emerge clearly when the basis of the problem is examined: the effects of a harsh environment, of remoteness and of political division, as well as of industrial decay or urban congestion. But these have not been examined in isolation and the studies that make up the series have been carefully chosen in order that useful comparisons can be made. Thus, for example, both the Mezzogiorno and Andalusia have to contend with the problems of Mediterranean drought, wind, and flood, but the precise nature of these and other problems, as well as man's response to them, differs in the two regions. Similarly, the response to economic change is not the same in North-East England as in North Rhine-Westphalia, nor the response to social pressures the same in Paris as in the Randstad.

The efforts which individual governments have made to grapple with their problems provides a basis for critical assessment in each of the volumes. For too long, solutions were sought that were piecemeal and short-term. Our own Development Areas in Britain provide a good illustration of this kind of policy. Of late, however, European governments have shown an increasing awareness of the need to undertake planning on a regional basis. The success or otherwise of such regional policies is fully explored in the individual *Problem Region* volumes.

When it was first planned the *Problem Region* series was thought of as useful only to the sixth-form student of geography. As it has developed it has become clear that the authors—all specialists in the geography of the areas concerned—have contributed studies that will be useful, not only for sixth-form work, but as a basis for the more detailed investigations undertaken by advanced students, both of geography and of European studies in general.

D.I.S.

St. Edmund Hall, Oxford

Contents

Introduction

Frontier regions

The political boundaries of Europe and the associated frontier regions have tended to be neglected as problem areas, and more tangible national problems such as urban expansion or declining industry have been given priority by individual States. Whilst most statesmen recognize national variations in levels of economic advancement, purchasing power, and policies for regional development, the European Commission concluded in 1970 that, after twelve years, there had been little progress in promoting trans-frontier regional development policies. Although every State could recognize its own peripheral regions such as West Germany's eastern frontier zone (*Zonenrandgebiet*), or the Eifel, or Alsace, very little progress had been made in the solution of the common problems that existed in the frontier zones. Some of the earliest efforts to solve common trans-frontier problems have come in the Scandinavian Northlands.

As economic union becomes more tangible in the European Economic Community, the frontier regions of the 'nine' are posing the problems that have to be solved if full economic union is to become reality. The boundaries still exist despite all the efforts to reduce their significance. Frequent halts at customs posts while moving between States brings home the continuing reality of the lines on the map. These lines separate distinct political systems which have given rise to differing economic and social policies which, in turn, have brought about discrepancies in tariffs, monetary policy, credit, investment aid, and regional development. Even more tangible to the citizen living in these regions are the marked variations in the levels of income and spending power that arise between peoples living only a few kilometres apart and farming the same soils or manufacturing the same product. This is always more apparent when currencies revalue or devalue. In fact, the whole basis of society—its institutions, such as the legal process and education, and culture—can change dramatically at the boundary. A telephone call across a frontier is an international call even if the caller lives near the frontier; in fact, all telephone calls in frontier areas are expensive because the region is peripheral to the national system.

The concept of the frontier region was first recognized by the European Commission in 1964 in consequence of the impact that the free movement of labour was having on the frontier regions. Prior to 1964 there were bilateral agreements on *frontaliers* or *Grenzarbeitnehmer* (trans-frontier commuters') movements between France and West Germany, and between France and Belgium. The frontier regions were recognized as zones up to 20 km wide on either side of the boundary. Since then other attempts to define these regions and their problems have been made, although the Council of Europe (like many geographers) was forced to conclude, in 1973, 'there can be few concepts as ambiguous as that of what constitutes a region.'

By 1970 the achievements in frontier regions were still few, although the ministers responsible for regional planning in the Council of Europe had met to discuss the co-ordination of policies in frontier regions. Frontier regions were recognized as one of the three most important problems that could be approached at a European level and used to illustrate the long-term objectives of a European policy based on an improvement in man's well-being and on the expansion of activities in terms both of economic development and of the quality of life. (The two other problems that were recognized were transport policies and mountain regions.) By 1973 the ministers were able to adopt recommendations resulting from consultation between States in frontier regions, and to establish bilateral and multilateral regional commissions concerned with joint action at the local level in frontier regions.

'The frontier is therefore an idealized line, a hypothetical construction, and its demarcation an attempt to confine within a single, rigid political limit realities which cannot be superimposed. The discrepancies between these systems and the frontier determine the frontier tensions . . . ,' declared a report to the European ministers responsible for regional planning.

In the Saar-Lorraine region there are all the problems of frontier regions that are outlined above. However, there are complications because the frontier region here is a scar of history. The Franco-German boundary has oscillated violently in this zone of cultural fragmentation. Therefore, there is no clear-cut division between the States: the see-saw motion of the boundary over the

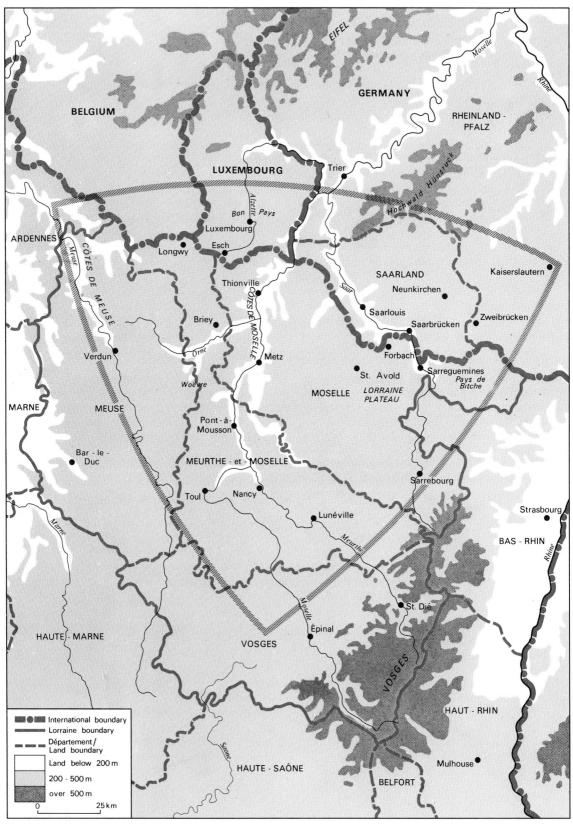

Fig. 1. Saar-Lorraine and the Saar/Lor/Lux triangle

The ossuary and cemetery at Douaumont near Verdun, built to house the dead of the long battle of Verdun (February 1916 to August 1917). Over half a million died in the First World War in the Verdun area, and the cemeteries are a grim reminder of a violent past

centuries has brought German traditions, language, and culture to Lorraine, and French influence into the Saarland. The war cemeteries, the concrete blocks and pill boxes of the Maginot Line, the barracks in the towns—all bear grim witness to the more violent episodes in the region's history. The oscillating boundary has exacerbated economic development, particularly during the past century, by changing the economic control of important resources and industries. While the boundary might have stabilized, the effects on the economy are still most marked, and economic colonization has not abated. The coat of arms of the Saarland contains the lions of Saarbrücken and Rheinland-Pfalz, the silver eagles of Lorraine, and the red cross of the bishopric of Trier, reflecting the vicissitudes of the past of one part of the region.

Yet it is not sufficient to consider Saar-Lorraine as a frontier region *per se*, with its attendant politico-historical problems. Once one considers the economic effects of the fluctuating boundary, it is inevitable that one is drawn into the other problems of the region. These are not unique and are common to other regions, although the fact that they are found on both sides of the boundary does make them unusual. The problems of the declining coalfields and the restructuring of the iron and steel industry and the textile industry can be compared and contrasted with those in North East England, North Rhine-Westphalia, and the neighbouring Franco-Belgian frontier zone.

A further complication is the fact that the problems of this region are not confined solely to the Saarland and Lorraine. Here the division is between four political systems: France, West Germany, the Duchy of Luxembourg, and, to a lesser extent, Belgium. For example, the problems of the iron and steel industry are as much the problems of Luxembourg and Belgium as of the other States, partly because the industry is found in those areas adjacent to Saar-Lorraine but mainly because economic history has brought about a complex network of company linkages that straddle the political boundaries. Similarly, labour migration involves all four States in a complex daily ebb and flow of people. Thus it is essential to include reference to Luxembourg, Belgium, and even the *Land* of Rheinland-Pfalz, at certain points in this analysis.

Saar-Lorraine—myth or reality?

Although a study of Saar-Lorraine requires one to examine the problems of a more extensive frontier region, it is essential that the region selected for detailed consideration is given some spatial limits. The most obvious limits are the administrative ones imposed by the States (Fig. 1). The Saarland is a *Land* or federal state of West Germany. It is a modern creation, the term first coming into use at the Treaty of Versailles 1919 and the present *Land* division in 1957. The province of Lorraine comprises the four *départements* of Meuse, Meurthe-et-Moselle, Moselle, and Vosges. This definition is unsatisfactory, but these are the boundaries of the political systems. The European Commission's definition of frontier regions would include the relevant areas of Luxembourg, Belgium, and Rheinland-Pfalz, but it would exclude the *département* of Vosges because of its distance from the boundary.

A more satisfactory definition is based on the regional planning strategies that will be examined later. Most relevant is the concept of the Saar/Lor/Lux triangle (Fig. 1), which cuts across frontiers and includes all the major centres of population in the region. This inverted triangle with its apex around Nancy and its base extending from Kaiserslautern west through Luxembourg and into south-east Belgium is the core of the region. Beyond the triangle is a fringe area which fades into the periphery of other regions such as the Paris Basin, Rhein-Neckar around Mannheim, and Alsace. Even the planning strategies seem to suggest that there are a series of forested natural regions that bound the region on two sides. These are the Vosges, the Haguenau and Pfalzer forests, the Hünsruck, and the Ardennes.

To some the region still lacks any definition: it is just a meeting of minds rather than the meeting point of the suspicions of society. Yet the psychological boundaries that most societies like to have block co-operation, and the concept of a frontier region must take this into account,

according to Strassoldo (1973). To some the region has a perceived identity based on the uniqueness of the juxtaposition of four member States of the E.E.C. This concept of regional identity is most forcefully presented in the work of the I.R.I. (Institut für regionalpolitische Zussammenarbeit in innergeinschaftlichen Grenzraumen), which has endeavoured, by its publications (including a newspaper supplement on the region published simultaneously by *Saarbrücker Zeitung* and *L'Est Republicain*) and its conferences concerned with the region's problems, to promote regional identity among the inhabitants and, more importantly, among politicians at all levels. The fact that the region is often referred to by many as the 'dead heart' to the European Community has spurred them on. Here is an area at the centre of the Community which lacks a common identity, despite the presence of many European institutions in Luxembourg. It is intended that the region considered in this book be the perceived region of the Saar/Lor/Lux triangle rather than any strict administrative grouping, and thus the limits of the area under consideration will vary according to the nature of the problem discussed.

One final comment that illustrates the problem of studying frontier regions is that the data bases differ. For example, the French census dates were 1962 and 1968 whilst West Germany's were 1961 and 1970. A variety of methods are also used to record frontier migration movements. Although every effort has been made to make data comparable, different bases and publication dates do result in comparisons being difficult to attain.

The components of the region

Physically Saar-Lorraine is the zone between the scarplands of eastern France and the Hercynian, Ardennes, Hünsruck, and Vosges mountains. The scarplands sweep across the region in three large loops of north- and eastward-facing, Upper Jurassic escarpments backed by broad dip slopes. The most westerly escarpment is the Corallian Limestone of the Côtes de Meuse, rising eastwards from the Meuse valley to uniform forest summits at 400 metres overlooking the almost flat clay vale of Woëvre. The Oxford Clay vale is 7–10 km wide at its broadest east of Verdun but is only 2–3 km broad to the north and west of Toul in the south. Much of the area has been drained for farmland although there are still extensive tracts of woodland. The population density here is low.

The second major cuesta is that of the Côtes de Moselle. The outcrop is very narrow in the north where the escarpment is actually within Belgium and Luxembourg, although it broadens out to form a broad plateau-like, gentle dip slope once the outcrop swings south at Dudelange. From Dudelange south to Nancy the 350–400-metre escarpment overlooks the Moselle valley although, in the south, there are outliers to the east of the Moselle, and between Toul and Nancy the Moselle traverses the outcrop isolating the Plateau de Haye. The plateau has several streams crossing it which drain into the Meuse and Moselle, the most significant being the Orne, the Fensch, and the northward-flowing Alzette. The plateau is more wooded in the south, but the summits of the escarpment are cultivated in the north where the large fields of the reorganized arable farms predominate over the karstic landscapes of dolines and dry valleys. The main significance of the plateau area lies in the minette ores found within the Oolitic rocks in two major zones: (i) that to the north and east of Metz extending from Longwy and Athus in a triangle to Dudelange and south to Conflans on the Orne, and (ii) the southern zone around Nancy.

Extending north and east from the foot of the Côtes de Moselle is the region known as the Bon Pays in Luxembourg and as the Plateau in Lorraine. The Bon Pays is an extension of Triassic and Liassic rocks into the Ardennes and the western Saarland. In Luxembourg it is the area of denser settlement and mixed farming, and contains the capital city of Luxembourg and the country's major towns. The Lorraine plateau extending east to the escarpment of the Muschelkalk is, because of its location and altitude, an area of continental climate whose varied geology results in broad expanses of woodland and a large number of natural lakes besides those created by subsidence from salt workings in the underlying Triassic rocks.

Beyond the Muschelkalk, extending in a series of loops from the Saarland into east Lorraine and then running north–south from Sarrebourg to Epinal, is a zone of Bunter Sandstones. The sandstones are sterile and covered in forests that surround Saarbrücken, and comprise the Warndt anticline that protrudes as a finger of woodland across the boundary south of Völklingen. They also underlie the forests of Pfalzerwald in Germany and Haguenau in east Lorraine. To the north-east of the Bunter escarpment in the Saarland, Carboniferous rocks, and especially the Coal Measures, are exposed along a north-east to south-west axis extending from Neunkirchen to north of Völklingen. The Coal Measures extend beneath the sandstones of the Warndt into east Lorraine to form the major part of the concealed coalfield of the Saar and Lorraine.

There are two more components of the region. First, there are the forested fringes of the Ardennes and Hünsruck massifs which form the northern hills of Luxembourg and the northern Saarland. Secondly, in the south and east there are the foothills of the crystalline Vosges mountains rising beyond Epinal and St. Dié and containing the headwaters of the Moselle.

These are the physical components of the region on to which man has etched his boundaries that ignore surface and subsurface geology. In the twentieth century few will notice, as they speed along the motorways, the variations in the physical landscape more subtle than the major escarpments and wooded zones. More critical to people today are the major urban foci and the city regions that divide the region into the spheres of influence of the major cities: Luxembourg, Saarbrücken, Nancy, and Metz. More apparent also in the region is the urban/industrial landscape of the coalfield with its mine colonies, pithead gear, spoilheaps, and, in the Saarland, steelworks. In the Metz/Thionville/Esch/Longwy region, the iron mines, the *cités minières*, and the works crammed into confined valleys alongside houses make up a characteristic landscape which transcends both physical and political boundaries.

The Saar-Lorraine area has been one of the most unstable frontier regions in Western Europe over the centuries. It is at the heart of the shatter belt between the German and French peoples and bears the marks of conflicts of increasing violence. The alterations of the boundary and related territorial changes have been most marked since the seventeenth century, being of greatest significance in the nineteenth century when the foundations of the regional economies were laid, and in the twentieth century, when the economies were twice rebuilt.

The history of boundary changes

The whole area was within the bounds of the Holy Roman Empire from 1056 to 1477 and remained within the Germanic sphere of influence throughout the late Middle Ages. However, in the seventeenth century the frontiers of the French kingdom were slowly pushed north-eastwards so that by the 1680s Saarlouis was founded as a French garrison town.

The Napoleonic wars saw the greatest north-eastwards push of French control, from a line running from Pirmasens to Saarbrücken, Saarlouis, and west to Longwy. Not only were the petty states that remained as enclosures in Lorraine annexed, such as the Duchy of Saarwenden, but by 1803 the north-east frontier had been pushed to the Rhine. The Treaties of Paris of 1814 and 1815 brought the fluctuating boundaries back into the region (Fig. 2). In 1814

Fig. 2. Significant boundaries before 1871

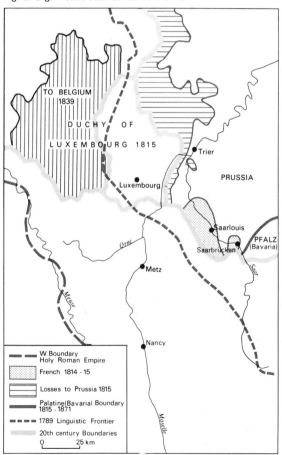

Fig. 3. Boundaries since 1871

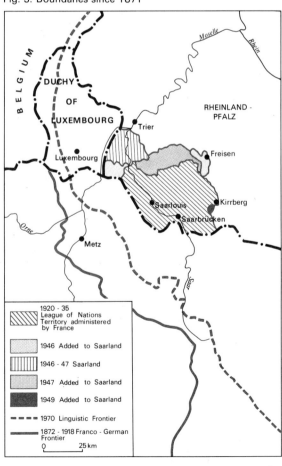

the first Treaty of Paris left the Merzig-Saarlouis area and Saarbrücken in France. However, these areas were returned to Prussia in the 1815 Treaty. At that time the Duchy of Luxembourg, which included the area of present-day Belgian Luxembourg, was also part of the German *Bund*. With the independence of Belgium in 1831, Belgian Luxembourg was ceded to the new State, and the Duchy assumed its present shape in 1839. Luxembourg joined the Zollverein, the German free trade area, in 1842.

A factor of significance for the economic development of the Saarland in the nineteenth century was the fact that Prussia controlled the greater, western part of the Saar. The eastern part of the present Saarland, including the towns of Homburg, St. Ingbert, and Blieskastel, fell within the territory of Pfalz which joined the Bavaria Zollverein in 1828. In this way the early exploitation of the coalfield was split between two States.

It was the Treaty of Frankfurt at the conclusion of the Franco-Prussian War in 1871 which brought about the most significant of the nineteenth-century boundary movements. Prussia annexed the imperial territory of Alsace/Lorraine. This did not include all of Lorraine but solely the area of the Moselle *département* (Fig. 3), and the action has been described as the dismemberment of Lorraine. After 1870 over 200 000 French left Moselle and returned to France. This area remained under German control until the end of the First World War and its resources were developed and exploited by the rapidly industrializing empire.

German capital was used to develop iron mining and the coalfield for the benefit primarily of the Ruhr and Saar industrialists. In 1881 a Koblenz metallurgical company opened an integrated steel plant at Rombas and in 1898 the Saar industrialists Stumm and Röchling built the furnaces at Uckange and Thionville, respectively. The communications infrastructure was also altered in the same period to serve the German markets. Today, the remnants of German architecture from this period are a constant reminder of the forty-seven years of Prussian economic domination.

During the First World War Lorraine became a battleground, as witnessed by the widespread distribution of military cemeteries such as that at Douaumont surrounded by landscapes that still bear the scars of war from the defence of the Côtes de Meuse and the fortress city of Verdun. Marshall Petain's order '*Ils ne passeront pas*' resulted in the loss of over half a million lives in the Verdun area between 1916 and 1917. Peace and the Treaty of Versailles brought the return of the Moselle area and Alsace to French sovereignty, although the administrative arrangements remained the same after 1918 and took time to adjust. As a result of post-war difficulties, wartime destruction and the loss of the labour force, it took until 1927 for iron ore output to reach pre-war levels. The Saargebiet, then a much smaller area than today, totalling 1900 km², was administered by France as a League of Nations territory (Fig. 3). The industries, banks, and insurance companies came under French control and the franc became the currency for the area. In 1935 the Saargebiet was returned to the German Reich following a plebiscite in which 88 per cent of the voting population voted in favour of reunification. The cultural, social, and economic systems were readjusted, and on 1 March 1935 Hitler entered Saarbrücken in triumph.

The Second World War again saw the advance and retreat of armies over the region. Moselle *département* was annexed and movement was restricted in the rest of Lorraine. Germans colonized the area and many French were deported. Over twenty villages in the Pays de Bitche were taken over for military training and 56 000 agricultural holdings were sequestrated to be Germanized after the war. The Saarland suffered several heavy air raids which destroyed factories and homes before the American forces began to liberate the area in November 1944. The Saarland now carried the scars of conflict: 60 per cent of the homes and 45 per cent of the bridges were destroyed, and only one of the five steel plants (the Röchlingsche at Völklingen—formerly French) remained intact.

French pressures to re-annex the Saarland grew as the Allied advance continued. In 1946 the Saarland, totalling 888 km² and containing 97 000 inhabitants, was annexed to France. In 1947 the Saarburg area was returned to Rheinland-Pfalz, and other territory in the north-east around Freisen was annexed. Two further frontier adjustments took place in 1949. By 1947–8 the franc was again the currency, and an official boundary was established between the Saarland and West Germany. French culture was re-imposed and became the teaching language of the new University of the Saarland. Even the Vatican agreed to remove the Saarland from the See of Trier.

The eventual return of the Saarland to the Federal Republic came on 1 January 1957 following the Saar Treaty signed by France and

West Germany in Luxembourg the previous year. The Treaty itself followed a plebiscite in which 66 per cent voted for reunification with Germany. However, several institutions remained under French control until the end of 1959 when the German constitution became applicable to the Saarland. France also agreed to buy a third of the coal output of Saarbergwerke and obtained the right to undermine West German territory for coal for 20–25 years in the Warndt. West Germany in turn agreed to canalize the Moselle from the French frontier to the Rhine at Koblenz, enabling the Lorraine industrialists to profit from cheaper transport on the waterway. This agreement must stand as the first instance of international co-operation to assist the region, including Luxembourg which constructed its own harbour at Mertert. The scene had been set for further co-operation.

Politically the Saarland became the tenth *Land* of the Federal Republic of Germany. The Saarland has its own legislative assembly which has control over police, education, and internal administration, and it retains financial independence by receiving all of certain taxes and a share of others. Investment incentives, industrial location, and regional planning are controlled at the *Land* level. In contrast, France is a centralized State and very few decisions of any importance for Lorraine emanate from Nancy compared with the decisions that affect the Saarland that emanate from Saarbrücken. Likewise, the small size of the Grand Duchy means that its Government is easily in touch with the whole State.

The economic significance of boundary changes

There are many aspects of the regional economies that have been affected by the unstable boundary between France and Germany as well as by other boundaries on the map. Linguistically, the area is split in two, although the western boundary of German speech/dialect has moved slightly northeast over the past two centuries. Nevertheless, the national boundary is not the linguistic boundary and there are very strong dialects present within the zones between the linguistic frontier and the boundary. Letzeburgisch, the

Luxembourg dialect, is one of the more widely known German-based dialects.

The whole development of the regional economies was affected by the long period of German occupation between 1871 and 1918. During this period the volume of iron ore mined in Lorraine rose rapidly: between 1870 and 1900, 145 million tonnes of iron ore were mined, of which 85 million tonnes came from the German occupied area, and between 1901 and 1918, 328 million tonnes, of which 244 million tonnes came from the German area. The occupation also accelerated the development of the iron and steel industry, in the southern sector around Nancy, and in the extreme north-west around Longwy. As the infrastructure of Lorraine was developed, however, it resulted in poor communications across the Vosges to Alsace, and between the French and German parts of Lorraine.

More recently, French occupation from 1945 to 1957, during the period of the economic miracle in West Germany, resulted in under-investment in the Saar Territory and meant that the Saarland re-entered West Germany as a relatively backward, undercapitalized industrial region. History has brought about a very complex economic interpenetration of French companies in the Saarland, such as Röchling at Völklingen, and of German companies in Lorraine, not forgetting other institutions such as the Ecole Française in Saarbrücken. The Saar's trade is still very much with France, with 62 per cent of imports and 56 per cent of exports by value being with France. The proportions of the Saarland's trade with Luxembourg and Belgium are 13 per cent and 8 per cent respectively.

The fluctuating boundaries and the succession of economic and social systems that have swept over Lorraine and the Saarland have left the area with a degree of interdependence that is not found elsewhere in Europe. Language and patois have much in common in parts of the area. The economic growth has been by industries linked across the States. However, interdependence is still viewed with suspicion by many, and the mistrusts of seventy-five years of conflict remain hard to allay, despite the many common problems faced by the region.

2 The Region's Problems

The problems of Saar-Lorraine must be studied in the historical context outlined above. The initial diagnosis of any of the problems has been a national one, although the solutions suggested are often very similar, if not identical. However, only in the past decade have there been any attempts to solve the regional problems in a bilateral or trilateral fashion. While many of the problems are interrelated, it is best for the purposes of this analysis to consider the regional problems under two headings: (i) those problems appertaining to economic activities engaged in on both sides of the frontier, such as coal-mining, the iron and steel industry, and agriculture, and (ii) the problems of other industries that are located primarily on one side of the frontier, such as textiles in the Vosges and the shoe industry of Rheinland-Pfalz.

Coal-mining

Coal-mining was first mentioned in fifteenth-century documents referring to the working of the exposed Coal Measures around Neunkirchen. Mining concentrated on the exposed measures to the north-east of the Saar-Lorraine field and in the northern tributary valleys of the Saar where adit mining commenced in the eighteenth century. The French occupation of the area during the Napoleonic wars saw a further expansion of mining, including some adits to the south of the Saar. The activity of the French was short-lived and was soon confined to an area south of the present frontier. The coal was used in the many small forges and glassworks of the region. It was in the mid-nineteenth century that the exploitation of the Coal Measures began to gather momentum, due to the combined effects of improved mining technology, the opening of railway connections from Ludwigshafen to Neunkirchen in 1840, the needs of both the Prussian and Bavarian States for coal, and the new blast furnaces being built at Burbach. The first French mine was sunk in 1856 at Petite Rosselle, and it supplied the spreading railway system. After 1866 the Saar Kohlen Kanal (Canal des Houillères) was opened from Völklingen to the Rhine–Marne Canal, enabling coal to be taken to the Dombasle salt and chemical works.

From 1870 the Lorraine mines were within the German empire, and all the mining in the coalfield was geared to the needs of the German market with very little coal being sold to France. Saar steelworks obtained concessions on the field, although the coal was unsuitable for metallurgical coke and used only for gas production. In 1918 the German mines in Lorraine were repossessed by France, and the coal was diverted southwards to replace in part the Ruhr supplies to the Lorraine steelworks. It was in this period that the French collieries first undermined German territory in the Warndt. The French mines recruited labour among the Sarro-Allemands although this supply dwindled after 1935. The inter-war depression years also witnessed a concentration of the industry into fewer mines in the Saarland. The 1940–4 period again saw a change of control and the exploitation of the French mining interests, such as de Wendel, by Reichswerke H. Göring.

In the post-war period the French collieries were nationalized, and the Saar mines were exploited by the French to make up for the short-fall of supplies in France. In 1949, 3·8 million tonnes of Saar coal entered France. When the Saarland was returned, the mines were placed in the nationalized organization, Saarbergwerke A.G. However, under the terms of the Saar Treaty, the French were permitted to continue mining in the Warndt (producing up to 46 per cent of the tonnage mined after the war). The undermining of German territory was limited, and a schedule for the withdrawal of French mining rights before 1981 was agreed. Today only the Merlebach colliery still obtains coal from the German side of the boundary. The treaty provided for a set volume of Saar coal to be sold to the Lorraine steelworks and power stations, although only two years later the French requested a cutback in the supplies of Saar coal.

In 1957, the peak year for coal-mining after the war, 16·3 and 14·3 million tonnes were extracted from the sixteen mines in the Saarland and ten in Lorraine (Table 1). Since then the two coalfields have been in decline, mainly because of competition from cheaper oil and natural gas supplies in the period 1958–73. The decline in coal sales forced the mines to begin extensive programmes of rationalization and mechanization. It was ironic that the decline in the fortunes of the collieries commenced so soon

TABLE I
Coal-mining in the Saar and East Lorraine

	Saarland				East Lorraine			
	Output (thousand tonnes)	Employment underground	Number of mines	Output/ manshift (kg)	Output (thousand tonnes)	Employment underground	Number of mines	Output/ manshift (kg)
1957	16·29	40 000	16	3069	14·30	26 000	10	2500
1967	12·41	19 250	6	5826	15·03	17 000	7	3510
1971	10·67	14 110	6	6499	11·51	11 500	6	4387
1973	9·17	12 500	6	6634	10·10	10 600	5	4446*

*refers to 1972

after a method of manufacturing metallurgical coke from the friable coal had been invented. Nevertheless, the demands for coke were falling as blast furnace technology improved. As the demands for coal have declined, so the production of coal has been concentrated into fewer, very large, mechanized mines. In 1974 there were only six mines in the Saarland and five in Lorraine. Only two new mines had been sunk in the 1960s, one on each side of the frontier, at Warndt and at Marienau. Although the underground-labour force has decreased, mechanization has enabled the output per manshift to rise.

The mines also obtained certain guaranteed outlets for their coal. New, large power stations such as Fenne, 225 000 MW, near Saarlouis and Grossbliederstroff, 220 000 MW, near Sarreguemines were built to utilize the dust coal. The latest coal-fired power stations have been built away from the coalfield at La Maxe near Metz. Coke plants have been developed and expanded at Fürstenhausen in the Saarland and at Carling and Marienau in Lorraine. The market for Lorraine gas had been extended to Paris, Sedan, and the Vosges, although it has been supplanted in recent years by natural gas (Fig. 5).

All these measures of rationalization in Lorraine were part of the plans outlined for the mining industry by the French Government. In 1958 the Jeanneney Plan envisaged a minor cutback in output until 1965. Faced with increased competition from oil and the potential expansion of natural gas distribution, the Bettencourt Plan of accelerated regression envisaged the concentration of mining into three pits in the east of the Lorraine basin: Merlebach, Simon, and Wendel. The labour force was to be reduced by 70 per cent between 1969 and 1985, or by 1300 men per annum. There have been two mine closures since 1970, at Sainte-Fontaine in 1971 (two years ahead of the planned date) and at Faulquemont in 1974. Folschviller has been

programmed to close in 1977. However, the mine at La Houve has been granted a reprieve until 1983 following the discovery of new reserves. Oil became a major competitor in the energy market with the opening in 1970 of the Hauconcourt refinery, which is fed by a 143-km long pipeline via Strasbourg. This now has a throughput of 4 million tonnes per annum.

However, the Arab-Israeli war of 1973 has forced the French Government to review its energy policy and to check the process of decline. The French coal reserves that can be worked without excessive costs amount to 600–700 million tonnes, of which 350–400 million tonnes are in East Lorraine. It is understandable, then, that the medium-term plan adopted by the Government in September 1974 foresaw the maintenance of output from East Lorraine at 10 million tonnes from four large mines until the mid-1980s, thus beginning to reverse the energy forecasts of the Sixth Plan.

In the Saarland there has been a similar reappraisal of the energy market, concentrating production in a few highly productive mines. In 1968 the Coal Adaptation Law enabled special assistance to be given to the areas most affected by mine closures. The supplies to France made under the terms of the Saar Treaty, which had been reduced, are now in demand, so ensuring that all the coal can be sold. Annual production is expected to be stabilized at 10 million tonnes, although only 9·1 million tonnes were mined in 1973. Thus there are two similar national approaches to the energy crisis which seem to merit common planning. The form that the initiatives took was a diversification of the energy interests of the mines. Saarbergwerke and Houillères du Bassin de Lorraine (H.B.L.) set up jointly operated companies to import crude oil from the South European Pipeline at Strasbourg via the 105-km pipe to Klarenthal in the Saarland. Here a small (2 million tonnes) refinery was built in 1967. By-products are then piped to Carling in Lorraine where petro-chemical plants have been located adjacent to the older carbo-chemical and coke plants. Another product pipeline then takes more by-products to Perl in the Saarland where a fertilizer factory has been opened.

The carbo-chemical interests of H.B.L. were reorganized in 1966 in anticipation of the advent of petro-chemicals to form S.C.C. (Société Chimique des Charbonnages). The carbo-chemical products from Marienau such as benzol, ammonia for fertilizers from Carling, and dyestuffs, were not produced on a scale large enough to compete with modern installations dependent on petro-chemicals. For this reason the marriage with Saarbergwerke A.G. in order to build the Klarenthal refinery was approved. Now large volumes of naphtha, ethylene, and benzol could be obtained, and the Carling plant was expanded, making larger-scale production that was more competitive. Saarbergwerke have also built a chemical-fibres plant jointly with Hoechst, the Frankfurt chemical firm, at Neunkirchen to employ redundant miners in an area where unemployment as a result of mine closures was very high indeed.

The arrangements outlined above have been approved by the European Commission and represent a genuine attempt at trans-frontier co-operation. However, the impact of the Arab-Israeli war in 1973 must cast doubt on the viability of any further extensions to oil-based co-operation in the energy market, and the mines must now look for co-operation in coal production and processing.

The iron and steel industry
Saar/Lorraine/Luxembourg is one of the great regions of steel-making in Europe. However, its location within the continent is no longer advantageous, and the industry has made several interesting adjustments to accommodate the problems posed by location. In all three parts of the region the iron and steel industry has played a dominant role in the economy in the past century although the industry's origins are much earlier.

Alluvial iron ore was won in Luxembourg from the sixteenth century, and there were small charcoal forges working the iron in Luxembourg as well as the blackband ores of the Saarland, first recorded in the same period. The exploitation of the minette (Jurassic) ores of the Côtes de Moselle began first in the north of the orefield, and from the 1840s blast furnaces dependent on coal, and later coke from Prussia, were set up;

these included Burbach (Saar), Mont-Saint-Martin (Lorraine), and Esch (Luxembourg). In the case of Burbach the intention was to gain a foothold in the German customs union (Zollverein).

The major phase of growth of the industry followed the annexation of Lorraine in 1871. Over 9000 hectares of the orefield in Moselle were annexed by the German Government who then permitted the exploitation of the ores. A further impulse for change was the discovery of the Gilchrist/Thomas, or Basic Bessemer, process for smelting the phosphoric ores. The ensuing three decades saw a number of new plants in the Saarland at Dillingen, Völklingen, and St. Ingbert, replacing the old forges. Saar companies were able to exploit the minette deposits in France, and they opened up mines and associated plants on the Lorraine orefield so that, for example, Neunkircher Eisenwerk founded Uckange. The links were not solely within the Lorraine area: for example, the Burbach furnaces used ores both from Maxeville (Lorraine) and from Esch-sur-Alzette in Luxembourg. By 1913 the Saar steelworks were receiving 3·6 million tonnes of ore and half a million tonnes of pig iron from Lorraine each year and a further 240 000 tonnes of ore and some iron from Luxembourg. The secession of much of the orefield to Germany acted, in due course, as a stimulus to the development of iron-mining and the steel industry in those areas of the orefield remaining in France. After a period of hesitation, investment flowed into the Longwy/Briey/Micheville area on the Luxembourg/Belgian frontier, and the area around Nancy. The exploitation of the orefield for the growing industries of all the States grew rapidly. On the orefield, 145 million tonnes were mined between 1870 and 1900, of which 85 million tonnes came from German Lorraine. Between 1901 and 1918 these figures had risen to 328 million tonnes and 244 million tonnes, respectively. The international pattern of the industry was strengthened in 1911 by the creation of ARBED (Aciéries Réunies de Burbach, Esch, Dudelange) from a series of smaller companies, with interests in Germany (the Burbach steel plant and Aachen coal mines), Lorraine (iron mines, e.g. at Terres Rouges), and Luxembourg (the steel plants at Esch).

After the First World War the German interests were sold to French companies, and some steelworks, such as those at Dillingen and Neunkirchen, had a majority of French shareholders. Other steel plants, such as those at Burbach and St. Ingbert, were controlled from

Luxembourg. In Lorraine itself, the production of iron ore took until 1927 to attain pre-war levels. In 1930 a new plant was built at Hagondange to supply the Renault car factories with special steels.

Further disruption came with the Second World War, but once the plants had been rebuilt and the mines restored, the region as a whole began to reassume its importance as a major centre of the European steel industry. Despite the expanding output of iron ore in Lorraine and the increasing production of steel throughout the region, however, there were signs of the ensuing crisis for the industry. In 1960 almost 63 million tonnes of the low-grade ore (30–33 per cent iron content) were mined in Lorraine but although output had risen steeply (Fig. 4), the labour force was declining.

From 1960 the position of both the iron mines and the steelworks which were dependent on these mines began to alter. The exports of Lorraine ore which had risen steadily until 1960 began to fall, owing to the increased use of richer, imported ores in the main export markets. Lorraine ores were not suitable for the new steel-making processes. The result was that the tonnage mined in Moselle fell by 17 per cent between 1960 and 1972, and the sales outside Lorraine dropped by 33 per cent in the same period. In Meurthe-et-Moselle the tonnage

mined fell by 31 per cent and exports by 48 per cent. The decline in exports was mainly in the sales to Germany (6·7 million tonnes, 1963; 3·3 million tonnes, 1973), Belgium (7·5 million tonnes 1963; 4·8 million tonnes, 1973), and the Nord area of France (2·6 million tonnes, 1963; 0·7 million tonnes, 1973), whilst exports to Luxembourg (6·3 million tonnes 1963; 10·3 million tonnes, 1973) mainly from ARBED mines, actually grew as supplies of lower quality ores within Luxembourg were exhausted. Only about 3·5 million tonnes per annum of Luxembourg's ore requirements are mined within the Duchy. In general it was those mines not tied to steelworks and those mining the deeper concessions where costs were higher which suffered most and closed, resulting in an average of 1830 lost jobs per annum in the mid-1960s. By 1973 the labour force in mining had fallen to 9000 although productivity had risen to over 32 tonnes per man shift.

Attempts to maintain the competitiveness of Lorraine ores were assisted by a series of innovations. In order to keep coke consumption as low as possible, it was decided to exploit only the ores with at least 33 per cent iron content. Enrichment procedures, which raised the iron content to 40–45 per cent before it entered the blast furnace, were abandoned because of their high energy costs. Only those mines that could be highly

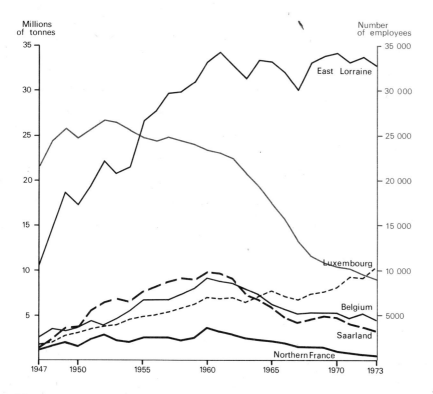

Fig. 4. The changing iron-mining industry (tonnages are sales to major customer regions)

TABLE 2
Changing steel-making technologies, 1960–73
(Percentage of regional capacity)

Process	Saarland		West Germany	Lorraine		Nord (France)
	1960	1970	1973	1963	1973	1973
Gilchrist/Thomas	74·3	54·2	3·0	72·0	40·8	0·0
Siemens-Martin	22·7	14·6	18·0	19·4	10·5	16·6
Oxygen	0·9	22·9	67·0	5·1	43·9	77·1
Electric	2·1	8·3	12·0	3·5	4·8	6·3

mechanized were retained. Following these decisions, it was estimated in 1974 that there were 1·5 thousand million tonnes of exploitable ore reserves, enough to charge the blast furnaces under existing conditions until the turn of the century.

The structural crisis of the 1960s affected the iron and steelworks themselves just as dramatically as it affected the iron mines of Lorraine. The construction of new coastal steel plants dependent on rich ores and imported coke, and utilizing the latest technology such as large-diameter blast furnaces and oxygen steel converters (L.D. or Rotor or Kaldo), struck at the viability of the Saar/Lor/Lux steel industry. For the Saar steel-makers competition from the Ruhr giants was strong within the German market despite sales syndicates, while in Lorraine the effect of the construction of the Dunkerque and Fos-sur-Mer plants has been to reduce Lorraine's share of French pig iron from 79 per cent in 1953 to 65 per cent in 1973 and of crude steel from 66 per cent in 1953 to 55 per cent in 1973.

To combat the crisis for the industry there were a series of options open to the steel companies. These may be categorized under the headings of technical innovations, company rationalization and mergers, specialization, and joint schemes. Technical improvements were one means by which these inland producers could improve their productivity and profitability. In the Saarland the producers were able to increase their output of both pig iron and crude steel faster than other producers in West Germany mainly owing to higher capital investments. Minette ore, which formed 98·7 per cent of the purchases by volume and 97 per cent by iron content in 1960, had fallen to 57 per cent by volume and 40 per cent by iron content by 1970. Imported ores, frequently brought by rail from Emden, had become the major source of iron. Saar coal, which comprised 80 per cent of the purchases in 1960, had fallen to 58 per cent in 1970 with imports now accounting for 20 per

cent of the purchases and Ruhr/Aachen coal 22 per cent of purchases. The lack of suitable canal communications, however, continued to hamper the Saar steel-makers.

The Saarland utilized sintering processes much more than the Ruhr makers and reduced the ratio of coke to pig iron from 974 kg per tonne in 1960 to 530 kg per tonne in 1970. The conversion of steel-making to the more efficient oxygen process has been slow, mainly due to the unsuitability of the minette ores. Nevertheless, the techniques have been improved and the oxygen process is increasing its share of the total steel-making capacity (Table 2).

Although the proportion of oxygen process capacity in both the Saarland and Lorraine lags behind other areas, and particularly the huge Ruhr and coastal plants, improved capital investments have reduced labour needs in the Saarland from 47 000 in 1960 to 43 000 in 1970 and in Lorraine from 97 000 in 1963 to 85 000 in 1972. The proposed closure of the blast furnaces at Neunkirchen could put 3000 men out of work by 1977. Today only 12 hours' labour are required to produce a tonne of steel compared with 21 hours' labour a decade ago. This still does not compare with the 7 hours needed in Japan.

The second strategy for meeting the structural crisis has been that of rationalization and merger. This has been a continuing process which has seen the emergence by the 1970s of three major groups in the region: ARBED, SACILOR, and USINOR-Est (Figs. 5 and 6). Whilst it has been impossible to create the equivalent of the huge Japanese or American integrated works, the companies have been able to create more economically-sized, although spatially-dispersed, groupings.

Prior to rationalization ARBED already controlled the Burbach plant in the west of Saarbrücken besides dominating the Luxembourg economy and possessing mining interests in Lorraine. The company had acquired an interest in the SIDMAR steelworks near Ghent in 1963.

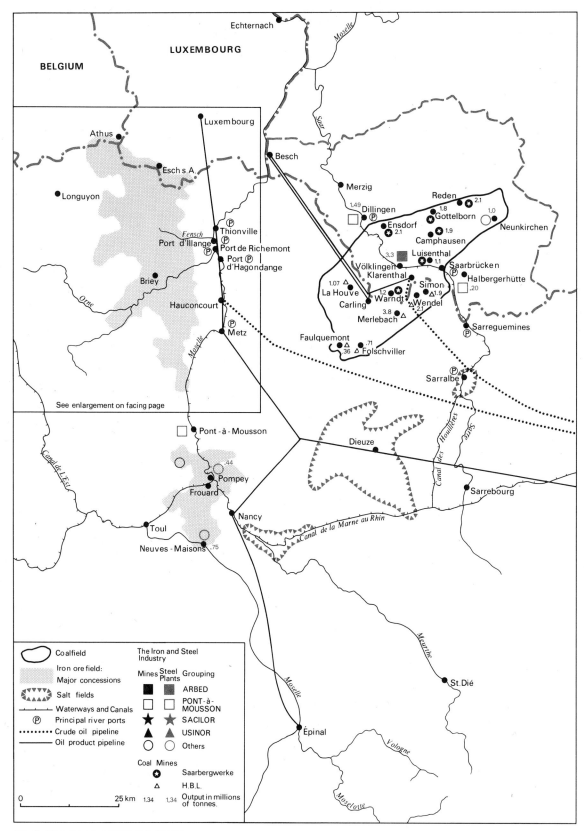

Fig. 5. Heavy and extractive industry

Fig. 6. The iron and steel industry in north Lorraine-Luxembourg

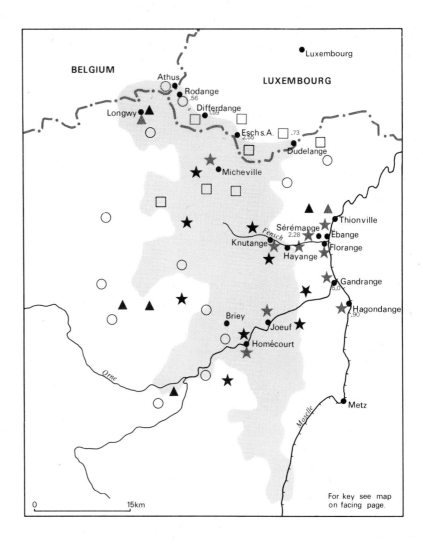

For key see map on facing page.

The dominance of ARBED in Luxembourg was increased in 1967 when it merged with HADIR to control four out of five of Luxembourg's integrated steelworks, the exception being Rodange. This merger also gave ARBED a further rolling mill in the Saarland at St. Ingbert. ARBED produced 5·3 million tonnes of steel in Luxembourg in 1973.

In 1971 ARBED and Röchling at Völklingen agreed to merge their activities in the Saarland to create a combined company, Stahlwerke Röchling-Burbach, which is now the largest producer of profile steel in the Federal Republic. This added a further 3·0 million tonnes to the company's total output. With 8·5 million tonnes of iron ore imported from Lorraine and 3·1 million tonnes of ore obtained in Luxembourg and some 3·2 million tonnes of coal purchased mainly from the mines in the Aachen coalfield, ARBED has become not only the kingpin of the

Luxembourg economy but also a vital component of the regional economy.

The largest grouping in Saar/Lor/Lux today is that of SACILOR (Société Aciéries et Laminoirs de Lorraine) which emerged in 1973 from a long series of mergers to become a major company mining 20 million tonnes of ore each year and producing 8·5 million tonnes of steel. The foundations of this group were laid in the post-war period when nine companies, including six from Lorraine, united in 1948 to create SOLLAC (Société Lorraine de Laminage Continu) with its steel and rolling mills at Sérémange, Florange, and Ebange in the Fensch valley. In 1951 SIDELOR (L'Union Sidérurgique de Lorraine) was founded by the merger of several smaller companies in the Orne and Fensch valleys. Three other companies, centred in Longwy and the Ardennes, merged to form Lorraine-Escaut in 1953.

19

Röchling-Burbach steelworks at Burbach in the western suburbs of Saarbrücken. The site is very confined by the residential areas, many of which house foreign workers who are employed in the works. The company is campaigning for the canalization of the Saar river so that raw materials can be brought by river rather than by rail

It was a decade before the structural crisis necessitated a further spate of mergers. In 1963, S.M.S. (Société Mosellane de Sidérurgie) was formed with plants at Hagondange and Knutange. SIDELOR and de Wendel joined to establish a new integrated steel plant at Gandrange. USINOR became the largest steel producer in 1966 when the company took over Lorraine-Escaut to create USINOR-Est with its plants at Longwy and Thionville. In 1968, de Wendel, SIDELOR, and S.M.S. merged to form de Wendel-SIDELOR which was also a shareholder in SOLLAC. The Lorraine steel-makers in the form of SOLLAC were very conscious of the need to establish links with or to invest in a coastal site. This was achieved in 1970 when SOLLAC was a major participant in the creation of SOLMER (Société Lorraine et Méridionale) with the object of building the Fos-sur-Mer integrated steel plant near Marseille; USINOR joined this agreement in 1972 despite having control over the Dunkerque coastal plant. The final phase of concentration came in 1973 when de Wendel-SIDELOR was completely reorgan-ized and renamed SACILOR. Now SACILOR is the majority shareholder in SOLLAC and so controls the greater part of steel-making in Lorraine.

The result of the series of mergers sketched above has been that processes can be concentrated and rationalized and the inefficient plant dis-carded. Hagondange is the most integrated plant while Gandrange-Rombas is the second major concentration. The smaller plants, and especially those in the confined valleys of the Orne (e.g. Homécourt), and Fensch (e.g. Hayange), and the eccentric location of Villerupt/Micheville on the Luxembourg frontier, have been fully or partly closed, with the result that 25 out of 48 blast furnaces, 4 out of 5 Thomas steel plants, and 4 out of 5 Siemens-Martin steel plants within the SACILOR group have been closed. Some 12 000 jobs were lost in the period 1971–5 as a result of rationalization in this group alone, of which the 3000 at Villerupt were by far the most serious because of the lack of alternative jobs in the vicinity. Other townships seriously affected were Homécourt, Hayange, and Knutange.

Placards on the hôtel de ville at Micheville/Villerupt illustrate the tensions that the structural crisis has brought to the iron and steel towns of north Lorraine. The slogans call for the modernization of one steel plant, the nationalization of steel-making, and the creation of the SAVIEM lorry factory in the town. The Renault subsidiary has announced its intention to open a factory in Micheville

It is impossible to discuss here all the mergers that have brought larger but still basically fragmented groups to the Saar/Lorraine/Luxembourg steel industry. The Belgian group, Cockerill, acquired the plant at Longwy-Rehon as the result of a merger in 1966. Other groups are based on international ownership of share capital. For example the southernmost steelworks in Lorraine at Neuves-Maisons has been controlled by a Belgian group since 1967, and Pont-à-Mousson S.A. with its small plant at Pont-à-Mousson, has an interest in Halbergerhütte at Brebach near Saarbrücken. The Dillinger Stahlwerke is partly owned by de Wendel, Röchling, and Neunkircher Eisenwerk and it, in its turn, also has a share in SOLLAC.

The effect of competition on the smaller producers has been somewhat different. In some cases, as with La Société des Hauts Fourneaux de Saulnes et Uckange, they have merged. This merger in 1965 was followed by rationalization involving blast furnaces on one site and processing at the other. The company, which is the only one in Lorraine concentrating on pig-iron production,

has since been taken over by USINOR-Est. It now uses haematite ores imported through Rotterdam and the Moselle navigation to its own port alongside the waterway. The small independent plant at Rodange in the extreme south-west of Luxembourg has merged with the sole surviving plant in Belgian Lorraine at Athus. Supplies of ingots from this plant are now used to supply the remaining rolling mills at Micheville-Villerupt following the closure by SACILOR of the rest of the Micheville works, and the move has led to speculation concerning a further merger. The works at Pompey have become one of the principal producers of special steels in France as a result of a ten-year modernization programme in which two oxygen converters and two electric furnaces have been installed. Whilst the output of 446 000 tonnes is small even by Lorraine standards, over 85 per cent of this is made up of special steels for tyres and machine tools. Brazilian ores are being utilized increasingly in preference to those from a mine nearby. At Pont-à-Mousson the giant French company, St. Gobain-Pont-à-Mousson, has specialized in the production of pipes and tubes, as does its small sister company, Halbergerhütte, at Brebach in the Saarland.

There have been efforts to maintain at least one iron and steelworks on the grounds of social need. The plant at Neuves-Maisons in the extreme south which was built in French Lorraine in 1873 was, by 1945, far from the centre of gravity of the Lorraine steel industry and its local supply of ore ran out in 1968. However, it was taken over by the Belgian group, Hainaut-Sambre, and its activities were underwritten by the French Government as production became gradually specialized. In 1974 the Government continued its support for the plant by guaranteeing that the Moselle navigation would be extended upstream from Toul to the works.

The third method of improving the competitiveness of the iron and steel industry has been the establishment of joint schemes, usually on a national basis. After the cyclical crisis of 1966, which reduced the demand for rolled steel, the Saarland producers participated in a work-sharing agreement. In 1971 this group then formed one of the four rationalization groups in West German steel-making (Rationalisierungs-gruppe Südwest), which included producers in the Ruhr and Schwabia. The object of the groupings is to encourage product specialization and investment, but not to provide production quotas and uniform sales conditions which conflict with the aims of the European Coal and Steel Community. The Saar steelworks, together with the Saarbergwerke, founded a common company to produce coke in 1970. Other costs have been reduced by the co-ordination of ore purchases in Lorraine and overseas, and by common transport arrangements. It is the Saar steelworks who have campaigned most strongly for either a Saar–Pfalz canal to Mannheim or the improvement of the Saar river downstream to the Moselle in order that the steelworks should enjoy the same benefits of bulk transport as their competitors in Lorraine. Work has commenced on the latter scheme. The steelworks have also established their own supply grid for liquid oxygen from Oxysaar Fenne.

A similar oxygen grid exists in Lorraine and supplies all the major steel plants in Lorraine in addition to the Luxembourg steel plants, the East Lorraine coal mines, and several other factories. The Lorraine steelworks also own two power stations, one serving the Longwy region and the other the Moselle/Fensch and Orne region. Finally there is a common research

organization, IRSID, located just to the north of Metz, which has an affiliated organization concerning itself solely with pollution problems. These two organizations are concerned with all French steelworks. ASSIMILOR, the employers' organization, was founded in 1966 and is located in Metz.

The one truly international venture in co-operation that directly affected the iron and steel industry was the building of the Moselle navigation. It ran first to Thionville in 1964, was later extended to Frouard and Toul, and is currently being extended to Neuves-Maisons. This European standard waterway has enabled the Lorraine producers to benefit from cheaper bulk transport and to construct three ports at Hagondange, Richemont, and Illange. Luxembourg has also been able to construct its own harbour at Mertert although, as we have seen, the Saarland steelworks have yet to obtain any benefit from the waterway.

The iron and steel industry is one of the major sources of economic linkage that exists across the frontiers of the Saar/Lor/Lux triangle, and the structural problems of the industry are common to all the four States. However, despite the juxtaposition of the industry in the States, the initiatives for rationalization and concentration have come mainly from the companies, rather than through international co-operation. The role of the European Coal and Steel Community has been to help heal the wounds caused by reorganization by means of a policy which is common to other regions of Europe. Nevertheless the iron and steel industry's problems do give the region a common identity and could result in further co-operation in the future.

Agriculture

There are common agricultural problems astride the boundaries due primarily to the impact of industrialization on rural areas characterized by relatively small agricultural holdings. In common with the rest of Western Europe the agricultural sector has been shedding employment throughout the century, but the rate of decline has been more rapid than in other parts of France and Germany. Agriculture employs 8·7 per cent of the working population in Lorraine (6·2 per cent in Moselle), 9·8 per cent in Luxembourg, and 2·4 per cent in the Saarland.

The area devoted to agriculture is relatively small owing to the extensive forests on the region's northern and eastern fringes which cover 47 per cent of the surface area of Vosges, 30 per cent of the Saarland, and 50 per cent of north

Luxembourg. On the cultivated area the land-holdings are small. In Moselle over 49 per cent of the agricultural holdings were under 10 hectares in 1970, whereas only 12 per cent were over 50 hectares. In Lorraine as a whole, 34 per cent of the holdings have less than 5 hectares under cultivation. These minute landholdings only account for ten per cent of the total agricultural land, however, and are concentrated in the Pays de Bitche. In Luxembourg the 9·8 per cent of the work force employed in agriculture are found mainly in the southern half of the Duchy. The size of the unit farmed is still small, with an average size in 1973 of 24 hectares, although the number of farms has been halved in the past two decades. Similarly, the holdings in the Saarland are very small-scale and, before land consolidation (*Flurbereinigung*), were divided into many lots. In 1970, 75 per cent of the landholdings in the Saarland were under 10 hectares. Land consolidation has reduced the number of small holdings, but the progress is slow, and 24 600 persons still depend wholly or partly on holdings of under 2 hectares.

To the peasant agriculturalists land is an insurance against bad times, and many have held on to their small holdings whilst becoming workers in the main industrial centres. In the regions where industrial work is most readily available, i.e. the coalfield and the ironfield, many peasants have become factory workers as well. The worker peasant (*ouvriers paysans* or *Arbeiterbauern*) is not unique to this region and can be found around many of West Germany's new industrial centres. In the Saarland peasants commute from the Hochwald Hills of the north, 25–30 km to the industrial centres such as Saarlouis. This movement is aided by the fleets of works buses that take workers to and from the villages. Many of these peasants have gone one stage further and abandoned their farmwork, leaving the land in 'social fallow' (*Sozialbrache*), although they might still live in the village. Over 46 per cent of the farmed area of 1960 was in social fallow by 1970. Others have rented their lands to itinerant shepherds who own no farms and just tend the flocks which roam the village lands. The effect on the landscape is one of partial abandonment; steeper slopes revert to their natural state while, elsewhere, trees are planted on the old strips. In northern Lorraine part-time farming is very common where alternative employment is available. Over 37 per cent of the *chefs d'exploitation* had another job in 1972. In Lorraine as a whole, 24 000 farmers have other, non-agricultural occupations.

Textiles

The textile industry is concentrated primarily in the Vosges *département* where the spinning and weaving factories were established during the nineteenth century, when they took over from agriculture as the main source of employment in the headwater valleys of the Meurthe, Vologne, Moselotte, and Moselle. The valleys were devoted almost entirely to cotton textiles, an exception being the linen industry at Gérardmer. The valleys provided water for power and for

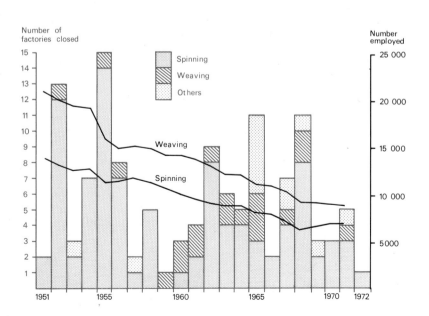

Fig. 7. The declining textile industry in Lorraine

washing, besides a labour force of full- and part-time workers leaving agriculture. Bleaching and dyeing plants were also to be found in the valleys.

The crisis in the textile industry can be attributed to several causes. The industry had stagnated during the post-war period, basically owing to a lack of commercial dynamism on the part of the entrepreneurs. This resulted in a lack of investment in new capital-intensive looms, so that by 1965 most of the machinery was over ten years old. Exports dropped, mainly as a result of foreign competition, but also because of competition from man-made fibres. Rationalization of output and modernization were needed, and this necessitated larger, more automated units. Between 1952 and 1972 the number of spinning firms declined from 44 to 23, and the number of factories from 74 to 42. In the case of weaving mills the decline was more dramatic: of the 130 enterprises and 180 mills in 1952 only 56 companies and 74 mills remained by 1973 (Fig. 7).

Many of the mills that closed were small but the cumulative job loss of the twenty years amounted to 11 000, whilst only 2 new mills, employing 130 persons, were built. Women still form the majority of employees in the industry. As a result more women work in Vosges than elsewhere in Lorraine. Employment in the industry declined from a maximum of approximately 13 000 in spinning and 21 000 in weaving until in 1968 there were 6300 in spinning and 9300 in weaving. Since then, employment has risen to 7000 in spinning, although the decline in weaving jobs has continued and only 8900 were employed in them in 1973. The decline in the number of weaving mills has been more dramatic: there were 19 400 looms in 1973 compared with 54 000 in 1950. The number of spindles has fallen from 1·8 million to just about 1 million in the same period. Salaries have remained low throughout the industry.

Productivity in the textile industry has, however, increased. Over 70 000 tonnes of cotton yarn is spun, although this is 5000 tonnes less than in the peak year of 1961. The output per spindle has more than doubled, and the region's spinning industry has increased its share of total French output. The output of the weaving looms has also increased in the past two decades, and the productivity per worker and per loom has trebled.

Firms have merged, the largest now employing just under half of all the textile workers in the region.

The vacated mills form a stock of industrial accommodation suitable for conversion to other uses. At least 42 of the closed factories remained empty in 1973 although the rest have been converted, some by firms using artificial fibres (this sector, too, is having problems as a result of the 1973–4 rises in oil prices). Clothing, hosiery, automobile accessories, and electrical goods are among the new products of the mills. The centres that have been most successful in finding new occupants for vacated mills are those which already have a broad range of functions and are more removed from the confined valleys of the Vosges. Thus St. Dié and Epinal have been more successful in conversion than Remiremont or Rupt-sur-Moselle.

Footwear

A similar experience to that of the textile industry in Vosges can be found in the footwear industry of south-west Rheinland-Pfalz, focusing on Zweibrücken and Pirmasens. In this region between 70 and 90 per cent of industrial jobs are in the industry which accounts for 40 per cent of all industrial jobs in Rheinland-Pfalz. Foreign competition, especially from Italy, and the high cost of raw materials, together with rationalization and improved automation, have resulted in a decrease of over 1000 in the labour force in the past decade. The higher wages paid by newer industries, especially those in the Saarland or Kaiserslautern, have attracted the labour supply away except in the more rural areas. The result has been that French workers have been employed in large numbers to replace the local labour force.

Mining, iron and steel, and agriculture represent regional problems that transcend boundaries, whilst the textile and footwear industries represent more specific, local problems. There are other industries in the Saarland, such as clothing and timber working, and in Lorraine, such as salt extraction, chemicals and paper production, which faced problems in the past decade, but their impact on the regional economy and employment is beyond the scope of this chapter.

3 Initial Responses

It is now possible to examine the responses to the problems resulting from history and economic change that the region has been facing during the past twenty years. However, it is apparent that the responses themselves can, and do, create further problems for the region. It is intended that this chapter should illustrate the inter-related nature of the problems and the responses, from the point of view of both individuals and planners.

The first response to the economic problems outlined in the previous chapter was that of migration. The problems of industries, coupled with the effects of migration, brought these areas to the notice of the various national governments who have embarked on economic development policies for their own parts of the region. In the course of execution these policies have brought about greater discrepancies between the principal divisions of the region. The increased national disequilibria, in terms of economic advancement and personal wealth, have brought into focus a whole series of other problems which are truly international and which can only be solved by international co-operation.

Migration and population change

An instinctive response of the inhabitants of areas having economic difficulty is to migrate from the region entirely, or to move within the region to locations with better employment prospects. In Lorraine, studies have been made both of the readjustment of the population and of out-migration. There has been a gradual shift of people towards the two major cities of Metz and Nancy which increased their populations by 1·55 per cent and 1·53 per cent, respectively, between 1962 and 1968 as a result of internal migration. This movement towards the two foci came both from other urban industrial regions in Lorraine and from the rural areas (Table 3). However, all the urban areas show a population gain by migration from rural areas. The net internal migration therefore follows the pattern of a regrouping of the population within the predominantly rural areas of the Vosges and around Verdun, in addition to the strong attraction of the two major magnets. A distinctive area is the northern ironfield and coalfield towns which have an almost static population. Then there are the small centres of East Lorraine and the upper Moselle and Meuse valleys, with strong losses by migration. Evidence seems to suggest that migration can be regarded as principally short-distance and taking place in a steplike fashion towards the major centres. The patterns of migration also suggest that there are three regions of interaction: Metz and the North,

TABLE 3

Migration changes 1962–8
(as a percentage of 1962 population for urban areas in Lorraine)

Urban areas	External migration	Internal migration			Migration balance
		Migration to and from other urban regions	Migration to and from rural areas	Total internal migration	
Nancy	−0·80	+1·64	+0·69	+2·33	+1·53
Metz	−1·33	+2·04	+0·84	+2·88	+1·55
Ironfield North	−12·28	−0·23	+0·50	+0·27	−12·01
Coalfield	−5·69	−0·18	+0·38	+0·20	−5·49
Sarrebourg	−1·29	−2·78	—	−2·78	−4·07
Bitche/Dieuze/Morhange	−2·40	−2·12	+1·45	−0·67	−3·07
Upper Meurthe valley	−2·30	−1·27	+0·42	−0·85	−3·15
Upper Moselle valley	−1·24	−2·23	+1·00	−1·23	+2·47
Vosges urban centres	−1·21	−0·14	+2·53	+2·39	+1·18
Verdun	−10·51	−0·76	+3·34	+2·58	−7·93
Bar-le-Duc	−2·32	−1·31	+2·01	+0·70	−1·62
Small towns of Meuse	−10·72	−4·41	+1·29	−3·12	−13·84

After I.N.S.E.E.

Nancy and the Vosges, and the Meuse towns focusing on Verdun and Bar-le-Duc.

While the movement towards the larger centres of employment is strong, the counter current of movement to the rural fringes of the urban areas must not be discounted. For example, within the Nancy urban area there is a strong centrifugal movement to smaller towns, such as Lunéville and Pont-à-Mousson and the intervening villages. By contrast, in the northern ironfield, the movements concentrate people in the steel towns and the sprawling iron-mining settlements (*villes minières*) of the plateau.

In addition to the internal movements of people within Lorraine to the main foci of economic activity and employment opportunity, there has been a much more disturbing exodus of people from Lorraine to other parts of France. Between 1954 and 1962, 7600 persons left Lorraine. This figure, though alarming at the time, was dwarfed by the 42 000 or 2 per cent of the 1962 population, who left the region between 1962 and 1968. Over a quarter of the outflow was to the neighbouring provinces, Franche-Comté, Champagne, and Alsace in particular. Only migrations to the Paris region and Provence-Côte d'Azur exceeded this exodus eastwards to Alsace. The main trend in migration to the neighbouring provinces was the familiar one involving movement to the large centres of employment: Strasbourg, Montbéliard, Mulhouse, Reims, Besançon, and Colmar. All of Lorraine, with the exception of Nancy, had a net migration loss to the neighbouring provinces. The highest losses were recorded in the upper Moselle valley where 16 per cent of the migrants were going either south into Franche-Comté or east to Alsace. A similar proportion, though a smaller absolute total, were leaving the coalfield for the surrounding provinces.

Over 80 per cent of the migration deficit with non-adjacent regions is to the Paris area, Provence-Côte d'Azur, and Rhône-Alpes where employment prospects, salaries, and life styles are known (or perceived to be) superior to those in Lorraine. All regions of Lorraine except the Pays de Bitche in the extreme north-east show a negative migration balance with the rest of France. Most out-migrants to the rest of France (55 per cent) come from the northern orefield, the Nancy region, and the coalfield. Thus the pattern of population movement appears to be from rural areas to the provincial centres, with out-migration as a final step.

Although the comments above refer to net migration balances, it must be borne in mind that there are a few who move into Lorraine. These are usually the job-mobile who can find similar posts throughout France and who migrate to the larger centres from equally large employment centres elsewhere as they gain promotion or climb the career ladder. Nancy is the destination for 28 per cent of these migrants and Metz attracts a further 15 per cent. There is a second group of in-migrants: these are the migrants from rural areas adjacent to Lorraine, moving to urban centres in the province.

Lorraine possesses distinctive demographic characteristics according to Clout (1972). In common with other industrial areas in the north it has a high rate of natural change ($+6·7$ per cent) but a large migration deficit to the more dynamic regions. The trend has been one of ever-widening out-migration. Both the more rural *départements*, Vosges (64 per cent urban) and Meuse (44 per cent urban), have lost population by migration since 1954, but by the 1960s all the *départements* of Lorraine were suffering from out-migration. In Vosges the numbers leaving had dwindled, but in Meuse the outflow had doubled in the 1962–8 period. The other *départements* also experienced large losses of population between 1962 and 1968.

The pattern of migration in the Saarland has many features in common with that of Lorraine, although, recently, important differences have become apparent. As in Lorraine, there is out-migration from the Saarland to the more prosperous areas of the Federal Republic of Germany. Until 1962 there was a small migration gain for the region. However, since then there has been a constant loss of people to the other *Länder*. In fact the Saarland was the only *Land* which still showed a net migration loss to West Berlin at the end of the 1960s.

The effect of the emigration of the young, dynamic element of the population has been exacerbated by the fact that, unlike Lorraine, the total population of the Saarland has been declining. The Saarland reached its highest population in 1967 and since then numbers have fallen. The decline would have been sooner and more dramatic if the influx of foreigners had not cancelled out internal migration losses throughout most of the 1960s. However, there was a further demographic factor involved in the Saarland: in contrast with Lorraine, a dramatic fall in the birth-rate from 18·4 per thousand population in 1964 to 9·9 per thousand in 1972. When this decline is coupled with a slight rise in the death-rate over the same period, the result is that the Saarland's natural increase of population since 1968 has not replaced the outflow. Since 1970 there has also been an increasing natural loss in population which reached 0·3 per cent in 1973–4.

Within the Saarland, the major urban industrial areas lost population between 1961 and 1970 when the Saarland's total population rose by 4·4 per cent. This decline was greatest in the mining settlements between Saarbrücken and Neunkirchen, such as Friedrichsthal, where the population fell by over 7 per cent in the decade. Other industrial towns, such as Völklingen and Dillingen, also witnessed a decline in their population. The waning fortunes of the mining and steel-making industries, and the drab environment with its legacies of the industrial revolution, have made these towns unattractive.

The converse of the situation outlined above has been the growth of small towns and villages, particularly along the major lines of rapid transit. Thus *Landkreis* Homburg on the main autobahn east to Kaiserslautern and Mannheim gained by 10·3 per cent in the period. However, there are areas such as *Landkreis* St. Wendel in the north-east where the commuting distances to urban employment are greater and the increases are much nearer the *Land* average.

In Luxembourg, internal migration and a declining birth-rate in the 1960s have brought about a general decrease of population in the north and east and a concentration of people in the outer suburban areas of Luxembourg City. In common with the other industrial zones, the steel towns of the south, being major concentrations of people, have lost population to the more pleasant surrounding settlements. On the other hand, there are no significant out-migrations from the Duchy, and it does form an island of in-migration. It attracts people from all the surrounding States, either to live permanently or, as we shall see later, to work.

Throughout the 1960s, in both Lorraine and the Saarland/Rheinland-Pfalz, the structural problems of the regional economies were increasingly evident and the demographic problems served to emphasize these. When these regions were compared with other parts of their respective States, it was soon apparent that they were falling behind economically. The Saarland had to make up for its years under French economic control, when investment in the heavy industrial sector alone was well below that being experienced in West Germany. When the Saarland was finally united with West Germany, the Gross Domestic Product per capita was 4·7 per cent below the national average. Rather than

improving, the differential widened every year until 1968 when the G.D.P. per capita was an alarming 22·5 per cent below that of West Germany as a whole. By 1967 unemployment in the Saarland, at 4 per cent of the workforce, was higher than in any other *Land*. In 1973 average earnings were still 1·4 per cent below the federal average. With fewer job prospects and a smaller variety of jobs to choose from, it is not surprising that many people living in the Saar opted for the good life of Frankfurt, Stuttgart, or München.

Likewise, in Lorraine, the standard of life has been falling relative to that of France as a whole. Other figures will serve to illustrate the disadvantaged position of Lorraine. In France in 1970, there were 748 persons per doctor and 2467 per dentist, but in Lorraine these figures were 953 and 2800, respectively. These averages hide certain variations because Meurthe-et-Moselle was more favourably supplied with both doctors and dentists; Meuse was least fortunate with over 1300 persons per doctor and almost 4000 per dentist. Telephones were present in 12·3 per cent of households in the eastern region (Alsace, Lorraine, and Franche-Comté), compared with 18 per cent in France as a whole; cars in 58 per cent compared with 60 per cent, and television in 73 per cent compared with 76 per cent nationally. Only 4 per cent of households had a second home compared with 8 per cent in France as a whole. Salary levels in Lorraine are below the national average for almost all types of employment. In the industrial sector, salary levels are 3 per cent below average and in Meuse and Vosges *départements*, 21 per cent below the national average. In the tertiary sector the average salary is 14 per cent below the national level. All these indices of social and economic well-being combine to indicate that Lorraine lacks the high-salaried growth sectors of the economy which act as magnets for population and linked industries, and raise the overall standard of living.

Regional economic planning in the Saarland

Official responses to the problems of the Saarland economy began in 1963. In that year the lowering of tariff barriers in the E.E.C. brought a halt to the creation of new industries in the region. Meanwhile, Saarbergwerke produced its plans for mine closures and redundancies which were to affect the mining settlements of Neunkirchen, Ottweiler, and St. Wendel. As a result, *Landkreis* St. Wendel was designated a *Bundesausbaugebiet* (Federal Development Area) and Lebach was designated a *Bundesausbauort* (Federal Development Town). At the same time Sulzbach, Neunkirchen, and Schmelz were made *Industralisierung Punkte* (Industrial Growth Poles).

The results of this policy were not very beneficial for the Saarland despite the supplementation of the aid from the Federal Ministry of Labour and the European Recovery Programme (E.R.P.). In both St. Wendel and Lebach loans of between 3·5 and 4·0 per cent, repayable over ten to fifteen years, were granted for buildings and the purchase of machinery. The *Gemeinden* were also able to offer further low-interest loans over twenty years with the result that up to 50 per cent of the investment costs were underwritten. Only about 500 000 DM. per year came to the Saarland as a result of this policy. More funds went into the industrial poles, mainly because the Labour Ministry provided loans for new industries settling in the region. The E.R.P. funds were mainly to help existing industries, although some were used for new industrial developments. The European Coal and Steel Community also provided assistance for retraining redundant mineworkers.

The West German economy suffered a minor economic recession between 1966 and 1968. The effects of this on the Saarland were more severe than elsewhere. Over 16 000 lost their jobs and, of these, 10 000 were miners and steelworkers. The net migration loss in the same period was 17 000. The reaction of the Federal Government was a programme to improve the service infrastructure in the Saar and elsewhere, and the passing of the 1968 Coalfield Adaptation Law. The law created the *Steinkohlenbergbaugebiete* by which investment premiums, tax rebates, E.R.P. and Labour Ministry loans would reduce investment costs by a further 15 per cent.

A development programme for the period 1968–70 saw 125 hectares of industrial land made available at St. Ingbert, Saarwellingen, Homburg, Losheim, Wiebelskirchen, and Blieskastel. New roads, schools, and a hospital were also begun as a result of this substantial injection of funds. As a result, new industries came to the Saarland in larger numbers, including Siemens who built four factories in the area. The Ford Motor Company built its second German plant on subsidence-free land to the north-west of Saarlouis. New tyre factories were proposed by Michelin for Bexbach, and by Kléber Colombes at St. Ingbert. Feasibility studies began on the linking of the Saarland to the West German waterway network. The outlook for the steelmakers was beginning to look more hopeful.

In 1969 there was a major policy revision in regional economic planning in West Germany with the introduction of medium-term, five-year investment programmes, the *Regional Aktions Programme*. The Saarland with West Pfalz was one of the designated areas (Fig. 8). The area to the north of the Saarland was included in the *Aktions* programme of Eifel-Hunsrück. At approximately the same time the Saarland and Rheinland-Pfalz both produced their own regional plans which included the federal calculations in their own broad strategies for regional planning.

Industrial development in the future would, according to the plans, be concentrated in a series of growth poles. These were divided into two categories. In the major growth poles, the creation or extension of employment opportunities was subject to 20 per cent aid on investment costs; these were Homburg, Saarlouis, Neunkirchen, St. Ingbert, and St. Wendel in the Saarland and Kaiserslautern and Zweibrucken in Rheinland-Pfalz. The second tier of growth poles could obtain only 15 per cent aid on investment costs for new jobs. These centres were Merzig, Nennig, Saarbrücken, Völklingen, Lebach, and Losheim in the Saarland, and Kirchheim-bolanden, Eisenberg, Rockenhausen, Lauterecken, Kusel, Waldmohr, Ramsteinbach, and Pirmasens in Rheinland-Pfalz. In the Saarland almost 40 000 jobs were created between 1968 and 1973, of which 25 000 were in new industrial units. As centres are deemed to have reached their development targets they are taken out of the programme and other centres are added. The major and second-tier centres in the Saarland in 1974 were as follows:

Major growth poles	Secondary growth poles
Neunkirchen	Lebach
St. Wendel	Merzig
Kleinblittersdorf/	Nennig
Oberes Saartal	Saarbrücken
Turkismühle/	Völklingen
Nohfelden	

Other decisions of importance have emerged during the last few years to further strengthen the locational attractiveness of the Saarland/West Pfalz region. In May 1973 the Federal Government decided to proceed with a plan to canalize the Saar river from Saarbrücken to its confluence with the Moselle at Mundung. This scheme was preferred to the longer, more costly, Saar–Pfalz Kanal from Dillingen to Saarbrücken and then via Kaiserslautern to Ludwigshafen. The new waterway, which will benefit the riverside steel plants

A new factory outside Neunkirchen. This factory, making chemical fibres, employs 900 people, many of whom were miners working at the Bexbach pit in the background

Ford Motor Company

The Ford car plant outside Saarlouis. This is the largest factory that has been attracted to the Saarland and it employs over 6000 workers assembling two types of car

TABLE 4
New industries in the Saarland, 1959–73

Kreis	Number	1973 workforce			Projected workforce
		Male	Female	Total	
Saarbrücken *Stadt*	10	668	287	955	2030
Saarbrücken *Land*	53	2564	3649	6213	8400
Homburg	24	5080	1382	6462	9150
Merzig-Wadern	15	3006	576	3582	4580
Ottweiler	36	1827	1550	3377	5580
Saarlouis	33	8044	2653	10697	17660
St. Ingbert	26	1734	1233	2967	4350
St. Wendel	27	2494	1390	3884	4830
Total	224	25417	12720	38137	56580

at Dillingen, Völklingen, Burbach, and Brebach, should be completed by 1983, at a cost of 900 million DM., of which two-thirds will come from the Federal Government and one-third from the two *Länder* in the ratio of 80 per cent Saarland to 20 per cent Rheinland-Pfalz. Autobahn connections northwards towards Köln, the Eifel autobahn, and west towards Luxembourg linking Dillingen and Neunkirchen, are under construction or being planned. The motorway and road building programme has averaged 140 million DM. expenditure annually in recent years. By 1972 the main railway network had been electrified, and container terminals were opened at Saarbrücken, Dillingen, and Homburg. Since its opening in 1968 the airport at Ensheim has increased its volume of passenger traffic and now has regular connections with Dusseldorf, Köln, Frankfurt, and München.

Despite the planning policies outlined above about 40 000 jobs were lost in the Saarland between 1960 and 1972, equivalent to 25 per cent of the *Land* workforce. This loss was greatest in the mining areas, particularly those of Ottweiler, Neunkirchen, and Saarbrücken *Landkreise*. The unattractive landscape, mining subsidence, poor nineteenth- and early-twentieth-century housing, and lack of suitable land made it essential for the new industrial growth points to be sited outside this zone of greatest need. Between 1967 and 1972, 653 hectares of industrial land were developed.

Since 1959, 224 new factories have been opened in the Saarland, employing 38 000 persons and, following expansion, this should rise to 56 500 jobs in the near future (Table 4). By far the most successful *Kreis* has been Saarlouis (30 per cent of all new jobs) with the Ford car plant which now employs between 6000 and 7000 workers,

and the COMOTOR factory manufacturing the Wankel rotary engine.

The effect of the new factories has been to alter the relative importance of the major industrial employment groups as shown in Table 5.

TABLE 5
Industrial employment by percentage in the Saarland, 1960–72

Industrial group	1960	1969	1972
Mining	31·8	20·4	15·4
Iron and steel	24·0	25·2	22·5
Basic and production goods	9·5	9·3	10·2
Investment goods	18·9	26·8	32·2
Consumer goods	15·8	18·3	19·8

Metallurgy, electrical industries, car manufacturing, rubber, and fertilizers are the main growth sectors, although the clothing and textile industries were expanding until recently. The growth in female employment has been very noticeable. While the increase in male industrial jobs between 1967 and 1972 was 10 per cent, the corresponding increase for women was 26 per cent. Female workers now number 49 for every thousand of the population, compared with 38 in 1967.

Investment goods have replaced mining and steel as the major employment sector in the regional economy. In fact, one worker in fourteen now works in some branch of the car industry. The oil crisis and the downturn in demand for cars in 1974 invites comment on the wisdom of using the automobile industry as the mainspring of regional renovation. Nevertheless, the growth rate of Saarland industry has exceeded that of the Federal Republic as a whole since 1968.

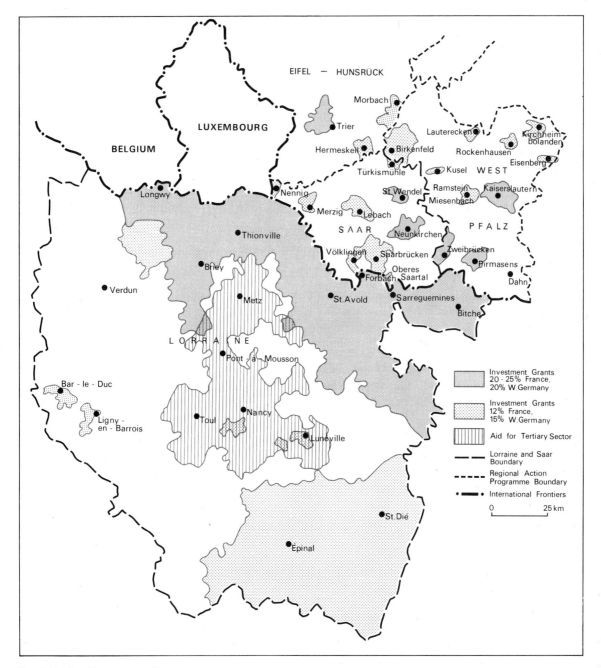

Fig. 8. Regional investment aids

Regional economic planning in Lorraine

In France, aids for regional development have been forthcoming since 1955 and these have been developed and extended by the French Government in the Fourth, Fifth, and Sixth Plans. At first this amounted to the Vosges textile region being designated a *Zone Critique*. Since then economic prospects in the Vosges have improved relatively, although part of Meurthe-et-Moselle was declared a *Zone Critique* in the late 1960s as the fortunes of the ironfield waned.

Since October 1973, regional reform has replaced the advisory CODER (Commission de Développement Economique Régional) by two assemblies having some decision-making powers over planning, including the power to carry out studies, make investment proposals to be effected by public authorities, and raise some tax revenue. The main form of aid to the waning economic fortunes of Lorraine, with its large area and population which is approximately double that of Saarland/West Pfalz, has been *Les Primes d'Adaption Industrielle* (P.A.I.). These were in force from 1964 to 1972 and governed all extensions to existing factories, as well as the construction of new factories. Since 1972, *Les Primes de Développement Régional* (P.D.R.) have taken over; the original zones were enlarged to their present extent at that time. In 1956 a regional development company, LORDEX, was set up to encourage and finance private investment in the region. The funds from LORDEX have gone mainly to Moselle and Vosges and very little to Meuse. The main recipient industries have been metallurgy and mechanical engineering. When the P.A.I. were first established in 1964 only the ironfield and its borders, the coalfield, and the *arrondissements* of Epinal and St. Dié were included. Between 1966 and 1969, as the structural crisis developed both in Lorraine and in the Saarland, the areas south of Nancy were added. The other major additions have been the areas around Sarreguemines, Sarrebourg, and Château-Salins, whilst centres such as Toul and Verdun benefited in 1968–9. In 1972 the areas around Bar-le-Duc, Ligny-en-Barrois, Etain, and Lunéville were added.

The present areas of industrial assistance (Fig. 8) fall into two categories: they are approximately the northern and southern areas of Lorraine. In the north, almost all the frontier region (comprising the ironfield, the coalfield, and the rural areas in between and south-east to Sarrebourg) is in receipt of investment grants as long as any individual investment does not exceed 10 million francs. Here an investment premium of 25 per cent for new factories, or 20 per cent for extensions, is payable. The second grouping comprises all but the western third of the Vosges *département* and five other small zones in Meurthe-et-Moselle and Meuse, where, for investments of less than 10 million francs a 12 per cent premium is paid for both extensions and new factories, although this is raised to 20 per cent and 25 per cent, respectively, if the investment is larger. For investments of up to 5 million francs the decision is entirely in the hands of the regional prefect, thus decentralizing some regional decision-making from Paris. The results of these schemes are shown in Tables 6 and 7.

Of the new grants awarded in the period 1968–72, 67 per cent were for new industrial

TABLE 6
Investment grants (P.A.I. and P.D.R.) by sub-region in Lorraine, 1968–72

Sub-region	Number of grants	Jobs created
Meurthe-et-Moselle:		
Ironfield	17	1960
Toul (1968–9)	3	290
Nancy (1969, 1972)	2	330
Lunéville (1972)	1	45
Total	23	2625
Meuse:		
Ornain valley (1972)	4	310
Verdun (1960–70)	5	420
Ironfield fringes (1968)	1	80
Saint-Mihiel (1968)	1	100
Total	11	910
Moselle:		
Coalfield	34	5286
Ironfield (1969, 1972)	5	308
Sarreguemines (1969, 1971)	3	700
Sarrebourg and Château-Salins	7	449
Metz (1970)	1	3470
Total	50	10 213
Vosges:		
Epinal area	34	6059
St. Dié area	28	2799
Total	62	8858
Lorraine total	146	22 606

plants. This figure was as high as 77 per cent in Moselle and as low as 48 per cent in Meurthe-et-Moselle. As in the Saarland the automobile industry is the major new industry, in terms of both employment and the value of the assistance. The greater part of the new employment was created by the establishment of the Citroën plant at Metz Borny in 1970, employing 3500 persons. Tyre plants, such as those of Michelin at Epinal and Kléber Colombes at Toul, are also large. Other large plants are some of those in the electronics industry: Philips at Lunéville and Grundig at Creutzwald. New textile enterprises provided almost as many jobs as the car industry but in relatively small factories.

The geographical distribution of the invest-

TABLE 7

Investment grants (P.A.I. and P.D.R.) by industrial sector in Lorraine, 1968–72

Sector	Number of grants	Jobs created
Mechanical engineering	39	3663
Automobiles	9	5180
Electrical and electronics	11	1880
Construction materials	7	646
Chemicals	12	965
Tyres	3	2080
Textiles and leather	27	4929
Wood and furniture	14	1177
Paper and cardboard	6	554
Plastics	9	1047
Others	9	485
Total	146	22 606

ments picks out the large number of enterprises that have located in Moselle. They have settled particularly on the coalfield, which has acquired a large share of the automobile (Girling brakes), plastics, chemical (Carling), electronics, and mechanical engineering sectors. Textiles have continued to dominate the Epinal and St. Dié areas; timber is also important in the latter district which includes the forested Vosges. In terms of the number of jobs created in the period 1958–70 as a proportion of the resident population, Vosges with 46 jobs per thousand people had the third highest ratio in the country; the other figures for Lorraine are Meuse 27, Moselle 18, and Meurthe-et-Moselle 13. Extensive industrial sites necessary for modern assembly-line manufacturing have been designated at Toul on a former aerodrome, Dombasle, Metz-Borny, Thionville, and Carling.

A feature that distinguishes the assistance that is forthcoming for Lorraine, but not for the Saarland, consists of the grants for the establishment of service employment introduced in 1967. The areas in receipt of these grants cover the two urban foci of the province, Metz and Nancy, and a broad region linking the two and including Pont-à-Mousson, Toul, and Lunéville. The *métropole d'équilibre* (counterweight city) of Metz/Nancy was designated in the Fifth Plan which attempted to provide counterbalances to the economic and social attraction of Paris. Although Metz/Nancy was a split *métropole*, the two cities were together seen to possess a large enough population to provide a varied labour market and a range of service activities related to a wide area of influence over the region. The idea of treating the 100-km Thionville/Metz/Nancy axis as a unit has resurrected the traditional rivalries that exist between Metz and Nancy. Union would make the area more attractive, but division and dissent, such as over the autoroute link to Paris, have remained. Both cities tend to view any plans with suspicion. For example, a plan to divert industrial employment to the north and service jobs to the south was interpreted as giving the best opportunities to Nancy. A rare example of integration is the fast rail link (METROLOR) between the three cities of Nancy, Metz, and Thionville.

Despite all the efforts to attract industry and office employment, Lorraine still possesses a large reserve of female labour, partly in the form of hidden unemployment (i.e. wives who are not registered as unemployed but who would take work if the right jobs were available). A recent report has noted the fact that the proportion of working women in the population is among the lowest in France (30 per cent). The establishment of further service activities would help to raise the proportion of working women closer to the national average (36 per cent).

Many of the trends in regional economic growth have been highlighted by a report on the Verdun area. The report stresses the increasing concentration of industrial and service employment in Verdun itself rather than in the broader region. Between 1966 and 1972, 1600 new jobs were created and 2200 others resulted from the expansion of existing employment. The growth sectors were metallurgy, food preparation, and paper, whilst iron-mining, timber, and plastics declined. Over 500 new jobs were created in the service sector, and most of these were for women.

Regional economic planning in Luxembourg

There is no specific regional economic planning policy in Luxembourg. However, there are preferences when it comes to establishing new enterprises in the Duchy. There has been a problem of adapting the labour force from its dependence on iron and steel. Aid is available for up to 15 per cent of total investment, and exemptions from corporation tax and various forms of rebate and depreciation allowances are available. Firms with large labour-force requirements are discouraged in the labour-short Duchy, as are those that cause pollution. On the whole, capital-intensive industries are preferred and they tend to avoid the steel towns such as Esch-sur-Alzette and Differdange, or Luxembourg City, and locate in the smaller centres, as have Goodyear tyres at Berg-Bissen (now the second largest industrial employer), Du Pont at Hespérange, and Monsanto at Echternach.

Disequilibria in the frontier region: the case of East Lorraine

Although both the West Germans and French made efforts throughout the 1960s to improve the economic health of the Saar and Lorraine, the success rate differs between the two. If the new jobs created in Vosges, Meurthe-et-Moselle, and Meuse are discounted, then only 10 200 new jobs were created in that part of Lorraine abutting on the Saarland and, of these, approximately 6000 were close to the boundary. On the other hand over 30 000 jobs were created on the other side of the frontier. In May 1972 *Le Monde* carried a report of a toy factory at Creutzwald whose employees left their jobs to work in the same industry in the Saarland where wage rates were 50 per cent higher. Energy consumption in the early 1960s grew by 80 per cent in the Saarland but by only 58 per cent in Lorraine. The density of telephones per hundred inhabitants in 1970 was 16·5 in the Saarland and 9·0 in Lorraine, both below the national averages, yet the discrepancy is apparent.

These broad indications of disequilibria are amplified if one considers East Lorraine. A research project has demonstrated the ways in which the million people in the southern Saarland form a more dominant group than the 300 000 just over the boundary. The infrastructure of the Saar has been better developed to cater for the greater numbers; whereas, for example, the roads in East Lorraine are poor and pass through numerous small towns rather than by-passing them. There is no large urban centre to rival Saarbrücken. The rates of industrial growth in the two frontier areas confirm the impression of growing disequilibria in opportunities (Table 8).

Industry has diversified more rapidly in the Saarland than East Lorraine. In 1970, 42 new factories came to the Saarland, employing 4700 persons whereas only 6 factories, employing 153 persons, came to East Lorraine. Decisions, it is claimed, can be obtained more quickly in the Saarland from *Land* civil servants than in Lorraine where the effects of a centralized political system are still hard to overcome.

As a result of new industries, wage rates in the Saarland had risen to 20 per cent above those in Moselle by 1969. With changes in exchange rates since then, the gap had widened to 65 per cent by 1972. For an employer in the Saarland the social service charges, assuming equal salaries, are 14 per cent lower than in France. In total the Lorraine employer finds himself having to pay 8·6 per cent more for the same nominal salary.

The most economically depressed area of East Lorraine is the Pays de Bitche, the peninsula of Moselle extending into Alsace, where agricultural employment still dominates, especially in the canton of Volmunster where 45 per cent are in agricultural employment. Many of the farmers here have become *ouvriers paysans* and cross the frontier to work in the factories of the Saarland or Rheinland-Pfalz. The farms are small and uneconomic and compare unfavourably with those in the Rilchingen/Hanweiler area across the frontier. Even in towns such as Sarreguemines the number of workers journeying daily to the Saar/Pfalz area has tripled in recent years to 1500, whereas only 65 Saarlanders come the other way.

Similar patterns of disequilibria can be found between Lorraine and Luxembourg, and between Belgium and Luxembourg. The result is that the social and economic systems on either side of the frontiers make adjustments to allow

TABLE 8

The growth of the workforce in selected industries in the Saarland and Lorraine

	Annual percentage growth		
Saarland 1968–70		Lorraine 1968–71	
Vehicles	50·5	Vehicles	22·2
Electricity	15·0	Chemicals	8·0
Metallurgy	14·5	Electrical goods	4·7
Metal-working	13·5	Metal transformation	3·1
Consumer goods	13·0	Consumer goods	0·5
Metal construction	11·3		
Machinery	10·0		
Chemicals	0·5		

Source: Les Dossiers de L'Economie de Lorraine, 1972, No. 9.

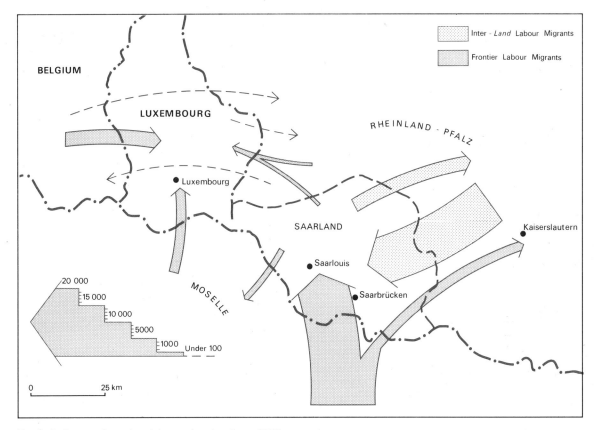

Fig. 9. Daily trans-boundary labour migration flows 1973

for those differences, and there is growing evidence of interdependence along the frontiers.

Frontaliers/Grenzarbeitnehmer

One form of adjustment lies in the daily ebb and flow of people across the boundaries to find work. The idea of *frontaliers* or *Grenzarbeitnehmer* is not new to this region, or uncommon in Western Europe. In fact, it provides increasing evidence of the economic disparities which split the continent. The flows of frontier commuters have varied, but they always seem to reflect the strength of one area and the relative poverty of another.

In the immediate post-war period there was a general out-movement each day from the Saarland to Lorraine. However, since economic reunion the numbers commuting to France and Luxembourg have dwindled, and each revaluation of the Deutschmark sees the numbers fall even further. Today, approximately 1600 persons journey for work to Lorraine from the Saarland. The figure from Rheinland-Pfalz is not known because it includes commuters to Alsace. A further 1400 persons, of whom 1300 come from the Saarland, travel into Luxembourg. Both figures are falling.

The Duchy of Luxembourg has been a major pole of attraction for frontier workers from all the surrounding States. In 1972, in addition to the German influx, there were 2900 persons from France and 4000 from Belgium (Fig. 9). The French commuters are workers moving primarily into the heavy industrial towns of the south. ARBED employs over 2000 *frontaliers* although some of these are Italians who came to North Lorraine, lost their jobs when rationalization took place, and now commute to Esch-sur-Alzette or Differdange to perform the same job. In Luxembourg there are large numbers of resident foreign workers and their families, attracted by the high salaries and the fact that Luxembourg is short of labour. The foreign-born population of Luxembourg includes 25 500 from the surrounding three States, although this number is small compared with the 33 000 Italians.

By far the greatest movement today consists of the 17 000 Frenchmen who cross daily into the Saarland and a further 2800 who journey to Rheinland-Pfalz. The numbers have risen by more than threefold since 1967. Over 80 per cent come from the cantons adjacent to the frontier and work in the *Gemeinden* on the other side. This is very easy in the case of the Saarland because on one side there are the higher densities of people in the Forbach, St. Avold, Faulquemont, and Sarreguemines cantons, whilst on the other side there are the major nodes of employment of the western section of the Saarland industrial V (Saarbrücken, Völkingen, Saarlouis, and Dillingen), with fast motorway connections to the other section extending north-east to Neunkirchen and Homburg. The Saarland companies often send works buses up to 40 km into France to collect the workers, despite a legal limit of 20 km. To many, the French are seen as the demographic replacements for those Germans who move to the more prosperous regions of West Germany.

The migrants themselves are (or were) miners, agriculturalists, or sons of labourers, and most are usually young and single. Many of them can speak German or the local German dialect and, therefore, do not have the problems of communication which face other foreign groups, such as the Turks. About one-fifth of the migrants work in the iron and steel industry, and others are employed in the building trade and in automobile manufacturing. A substantial number of women are employed in the service sector, especially in Saarbrücken.

Trans-frontier industrial investments
Another way in which the disequilibria have been accommodated is by factory building and investment across the boundaries. This has been encouraged by the respective Governments for several reasons and, again, it is not without precedent. History has brought about a pattern of cross-boundary investment during phases of occupation and many relics remain. The French domination of the Saarland economy in the post-war period is still manifest in French participation in the steel companies, the banks in Saarbrücken, and the bilingual school. However, the dominant role of the buoyant German economy, and the growing labour shortages in both the Saarland and Rheinland-Pfalz, have brought an increasing number of companies into Lorraine where labour is more plentiful and cheaper to hire. This economic colonization of the Moselle *département* in particular has been aided partly by the bilingual status of the eastern half of Moselle, where most of the firms are to be found, and partly by industrial adaptation grants. Only 12 of the 67 German firms which located in Moselle between 1956 and 1970 were set up west of the linguistic boundary. Grundig at Creutzwald and Continental Tyres at Sarreguemines represent two German investments just over the boundary.

Not all the investments in Lorraine are German. By 1973 companies with more than 20 per cent foreign control were to be found throughout Lorraine, employing 55 000 persons or 15 per cent of the industrial workforce. Between 1967 and 1973 the numbers had grown by 11 000. Of the 55 000 employees, over 20 000 work for 17 German companies and 15 700 for Belgian/Luxembourg firms, i.e. 70 per cent work for companies investing across the frontier. It is the German investment which has increased most: over 5600 of the jobs created since 1967, or half the jobs created by foreign investment, have come from German companies. Their major interests are in metal-working which accounted for 87 per cent of both German and Benelux employment in the region. In the case

TABLE 9
Foreign investment in Lorraine, 1972

Industry	Country of owner companies				Total workforce	
	West Germany		Belgium/Luxembourg			
	Number employed	Percentage	Number employed	Percentage	Number	Percentage
Food	—	—	—	—	829	1·7
Chemicals	1632	9·0	1712	11·0	4868	9·9
Metal-working	15 914	87·5	13 687	87·7	37 280	75·7
Construction materials	254	1·4	207	1·3	547	1·1
Textiles and leather	148	0·8	—	—	4660	9·4
Wood, paper, printing	237	1·3	—	—	838	1·7
Tertiary	—	—	—	—	236	0·5
Total	18 185	100	15 606	100	49 258	100

of Belgium/Luxembourg much of the investment in metal-working is accounted for by ARBED's interests. Since metal-working is declining within Lorraine it is ironic that employment by foreign companies from Belgium, Luxembourg, and West Germany in this sector is growing. This is because the investments are in modern processes and plants. Investments in the chemical industry are in the traditional processes of Lorraine: salt, chlorine, carbo-chemicals, and rubber.

Some 52 per cent of all foreign-paid wages in Lorraine are paid within the *département* of Moselle. Metal-working accounts for all but 5000 of the 26 000 employed by the 32 foreign companies. Meurthe-et-Moselle, which had the largest numbers of foreign-paid employees in 1967, now has 18 000 working for 33 foreign companies. In contrast with Moselle, these tend to work for companies in which the share of foreign capital is lower than average. It is also noticeable that Belgian/Luxembourg investment dominates here and that there is only one West German investment in Lunéville, the Trailor lorry plant. Foreign investment in the remaining two *départements* is small with that in Vosges growing and Meuse having a declining share.

Although attention has been focused on foreign investment in Lorraine, there are examples of the reverse procedure, although complete statistics such as those provided by INSEE for Table 9 are not available. In the Saarland, factories such as those of COMOTOR near Saarlouis, Michelin employing 1500 at Homburg, or Kléber Colombes with over 1000 employees in St. Ingbert, represent examples of recent French investments. Some firms even recruit Frenchmen to work in their German factories.

Second homes as trans-frontier investments

A second form of economic colonization is that of second-home ownership. The lower prices of farm houses in Lorraine and the absence of commuter villages in many parts of the province, together with the greater purchasing power of the Deutschmark, has enabled many West Germans to buy property in Lorraine. These are not seasonal homes as in other, more southerly parts of France, but weekend retreats. It is also a phenomenon which, as far as the Germans are concerned, is confined to the eastern half of Lorraine, where the German patois is spoken and where there are major recreational zones, including the Vosges mountains. It was estimated in 1973 that 70 per cent of the volume of land sales in Moselle was to West Germans, and that

over 2000 second homes had been built, without permits, by foreigners. The main areas where homes were bought were in the lake areas around Sarrebourg and Mittersheim. In some localities the invasion has met with resistance, as at Haspelschiedt, where the municipality refuses to sell land to Germans: they may only rent it. The phenomenon is not confined to the upper socio-economic groups and, as has been found in other studies in West Germany, second homes can take the form of permanently parked caravans. In fact, some of the large camping and recreational centres have areas permanently reserved for German caravans.

The growth of cities

A study of the four urban foci of the region illustrates the different levels of economic and social development attained in the region's national subdivisions. This is appropriate, because Saar/Lor/Lux is made up of four city regions and not one. Many of West Europe's problem frontier regions fall into one of two categories. There are those regions where there is a dominating city close to the boundary to act as a focus. This is most marked in the *Regio Basiliensis* focusing on Basel which provides the heart of a tri-State region; Geneva is another example. Then there are frontier regions where there is no large urban nucleus nearby and where there is, therefore, a natural tendency to look away from the boundary as has been the case along the Pyrenees. Such a frontier region may be regarded as a diminishing no-man's land between two major urban systems as is the case of the Dutch-German frontier in the Lower Rhineland. For Saar-Lorraine the evolution of the national territories and the distribution of resources have combined to bring about a multi-centred region which some see as resembling the Randstad region of the Netherlands. Although attention is focused on four urban centres—Luxembourg, Saarbrücken, Nancy, and Metz—one could equally include Trier and perhaps Kaiserslautern, as their urban influence extends into the northern and eastern fringes of the region.

Luxembourg

The city of Luxembourg must be regarded as the regional capital if Saar/Lor/Lux is to justify its claim to being at the heart of the Common Market. Luxembourg City is the capital of the Duchy and has a long tradition as an administrative centre which has been used by the growing European institutions. Luxembourg contains some of the offices of the European Commission,

Amt für Wirtschafts- und Verkehrsförderung, Saarbrücken

Above: Central Saarbrücken. Note the large number of modern buildings and the riverside urban motorway providing easy access to the city. The *Land* government offices are to the right (south) of the river Saar

Right: Luxembourg City, one of the cities that lays claim to the status of regional capital

Luxembourg Embassy

most of which moved to Brussels in 1968. The European Statistical Office, the European Investment Bank, and the Court of Justice—all part of the Common Market administration—are still in Luxembourg. The city sees itself as a nascent West European capital partly because it is the most central of the three cities that can lay claim to this status by reason of their European institutions: Brussels, Luxembourg, and Strasbourg.

Luxembourg is also a major financial centre, growing rapidly in status. One of the explanations lies in the fact that a law was passed in 1929 exempting holding companies from capital gains tax and exchange controls. The result has been that a large number of banks have been attracted to the city, all benefiting from the tax exemptions and proximity to European decision-making and investment. In 1971 Luxembourg had major offices of forty-four banks, and the growth rate in bank employment was 13 per cent compared with 1 per cent for industry. By late 1974 there were seventy-nine banks whose assets had risen by 63 per cent in the previous year. The new glass-walled monuments to international banking are rising along the boulevards surrounding the old city in which are now employed 4 per cent of the working population.

Luxembourg is the nodal point of the Duchy, but communications with its neighbours are still relatively poor. No autoroute traverses the frontiers, although the links are planned. There is only one short length of motorway between Esch-sur-Alzette and the Capital, and a southern ring motorway is under construction. Luxembourg, however, possesses the region's only truly international airport at Findel.

Centrality in Western Europe underlies all Luxembourg's claims to being the regional capital. Paris, Rotterdam, and the Ruhr are all 300 km away; Hamburg, London, and München approximately 500 km away. However, Luxembourg City is peripheral to a region made up of such cities and as a centre of employment and services its own hinterland covers the Duchy, parts of Belgium, northern Lorraine, and western Saar-Pfalz.

Saarbrücken

Saarbrücken is, politically, the most recently elevated of all four centres. It is the capital of the *Land* and, following local government reform, it now houses 223 000 people within the new city limits. The federal governmental functions are grouped into six ministries, and a further thirty-three governmental organizations have their regional offices in the city. The city also contains a French consulate among the thirteen consulates and several French banks. Saarbrücken is a focus for service employment, with 37 per cent of the working population in the tertiary sector and a further 33 per cent in trade and transport. In 1974 a genuinely regional bank was established in the city when the Commerz-Kredit-Bank was founded to promote German–French trade in the region. The financial basis of the bank, however (60 per cent German and 35 per cent French capital), reflects the dominance of the former in the regional trade pattern.

Saarbrücken's links with the rest of Europe are slightly superior to Luxembourg's. It is on the 'Goethe Express' train link between Paris and Frankfurt, whereas Luxembourg can be reached only by changing trains. By 1977 the motorway to Paris will have been completed. However, there is the ever-present threat that the reform of regional government might result in the amalgamation of the Saarland with Rheinland-Pfalz and a resultant loss of status as capital to Mainz. Saarbrücken's sphere of influence extends into eastern Lorraine and beyond the eastern boundaries of the Saarland, but, like Luxembourg, it can hardly claim to be more than a centre for one corner of the triangle.

Nancy

Nancy, with 258 000 inhabitants is the provincial capital of Lorraine, having first risen to prominence in the eighteenth century as capital of an independent State and, later (with the arrival of emigrés from Moselle in 1871), as a garrison city. Being part of a centralized State, few regional functions have been permitted to grow up within the city. Nevertheless, service employment accounts for 66 per cent of the labour force. The city possesses a regional stock exchange, a university, and the headquarters of several major companies represented in the region.

Nancy's hinterland, thanks to the odd shape of Meurthe-et-Moselle, extends from the international boundary in the north to Epinal in the south and from Bar-le-Duc in the west to Sarrebourg in the east. In fact, it commands more of the region's core than either Luxembourg or Saarbrücken. However, Nancy is located to the south of the triangle and it is not a nodal point for future communications. While it is situated on the rail and road routes east from Paris to Strasbourg and at the southern limit of the Moselle autoroute, it is off the course of the new autoroute linking Paris and Frankfurt via Metz. This decision was seen by southern Lorraine as a rebuff for the city, which has vied with Metz for regional dominance.

Metz

Metz is the focus of industrial Lorraine and was, in 1789, the premier city of Lorraine. However, between 1871 and 1918 the city declined to the status of a small centre of a frontier province, having lost part of its zone of influence. The architectural relics of this period are German in style and are epitomized by the baroque railway station. Today Metz is the *chef lieu* of the *département* and the military centre of the region. It also houses important business head offices, such as those of SACILOR, and 59 per cent of the working population are in the tertiary sector. Metz has had more success than Nancy in attracting new industries, such as Citroën at Borny and the Hauconcourt oil refinery. It also possesses a river port of increasing importance and better transport links with the Saarland than its southern rival. However, its sphere of influence is smaller and scarcely extends across the boundaries or into east Lorraine.

It is understandable that the French Government, when faced with the twin cities of Metz and Nancy competing for regional dominance decided in 1964 to make Metz/Nancy a single *métropole d'équilibre*. In 1966 an O.R.E.A.M. (Organisation pour l'étude d'aménagement d'aire métropolitaine) was founded in Pont-à-Mousson charged with the task of developing the 4000 km² extending 100 km from Thionville to Nancy. The O.R.E.A.M. proposed four alternative strategies for the new *métropole*: (i) the rejection of the idea and continued separate development of Nancy and Metz; (ii) the development of a mid-point centre around Pont-à-Mousson; (iii) the division of functions between services in the south and manufacturing in the north without regard to the frontier; and (iv) the growth of a city region in harmony with neighbouring regions, so that the services and functions of the area would be at 'a truly European level'. The psychological distance between the three urban/industrial cornerstones of the region—Metz/Nancy, Saarbrücken/Saarland, and Luxembourg—was not underestimated in the recommendation and acceptance in 1970 of the fourth strategy.

4 International Strategies

It is now possible to examine the region as a whole and the proposals that have been made for the future development of an entity called Saar/Lor/Lux at the heart of the E.E.C., as opposed to those that approach the problems from a nationalistic viewpoint. There are two levels of initiative which are being co-ordinated: the initiatives which result from bilateral and trilateral agreements, and the international proposals emanating from the European Commission and the Council of Europe.

The canalization of the Moselle

The earliest initiatives that brought about co-operation between the States came with the long-proposed scheme to canalize the Moselle. The scheme was first investigated in 1953, but no real progress came until the signing of the Saar Treaty in 1956. The initial agreement was for the canalization of the river as far as Thionville and for the inclusion of a port for Luxembourg at Mertert. The negotiations were not easy, but since the opening of the sections to Thionville and Metz in 1964, the canal has justified the predictions of its French backers. Since 1964 the waterway has been extended upstream to Frouard and is almost complete to Toul. The final extensions to Neuves-Maisons on the Moselle are under construction, although slightly behind schedule. A short stretch of the river Meurthe is planned for canalization as far as Dombasle. New harbours have been built at Richemont (for SACILOR) and Metz to take the larger barges that now use the waterway. The waterway is governed by an international commission in Trier.

The benefits of the canal cannot be under-estimated. Traffic crossing the boundary into and out of France at Koenigsmacker amounted to 7·5 million tonnes in 1971, although it fell back to 6·9 million tonnes in 1972. The traffic of the ports of Thionville-Illage (3·0 million tonnes, 1972) and Mondelange-Richemont (2·3 million tonnes) is made up almost entirely of raw materials for, and the products of, the iron and steel industry. J. E. Martin (1974) has shown how the tonnage handled by these ports has been affected by the policies of the French and German railways who were permitted to reduce their tariffs on cargoes of coal and coke moving from the Ruhr to Lorraine. The new competitive rate which was charged for cargoes going to the Orne and Fensch plants has meant that more coal still crosses into France by rail than on the waterway designed to take the traffic. Further, the plants of north Lorraine have not benefited from these special rates, so that the cost of moving coal to Longwy and Villerupt is higher. The scheme for taking coke by canal and rail to Luxembourg via Mertert had not been used by 1970. In conclusion the canal has increased the volume of trade, but because of railway competition supported by the national governments, the volume of traffic has been kept artificially low.

The port of Metz is the latest successful development. It was opened in 1971 and already handled half a million tonnes of traffic by 1972. The main cargo, which comprises 98 per cent of exports, is grain destined primarily for West Germany. It remains to be seen whether the more southerly ports will benefit as greatly as those already built.

The addition of the Saar navigation will enhance the regional network but will not necessitate international co-operation. It will probably be the death knell for the small Canal des Houillères linking the Saar with the Rhine–Marne Canal. Traffic on the Canal des Houillères has already fallen by 50 per cent in the past decade and only totals 700 000 tonnes.

A regional commercial centre

A more recent attempt to give the region a common outlook has been by the efforts of interested parties on both sides of the Franco-German boundary to create a new commercial centre. It has arisen out of co-operation between the societies promoting economic development in Saarbrücken and Sarreguemines and represents an attempt to create a point around which the regional trade can focus. Other frontier regions experiencing disequilibria in economic opportunities and massive daily migrations of workers often have a major economic focus to act as the centre to the whole region (page 37). The C.E.C.O.F.A. (Centre Economique et Commercial Franco-Allemande) is a much smaller project designed to employ only 5000 persons. It is intended to be located between Saarbrücken and Forbach, astride the boundary but also on the motorway linking Lorraine with the Saarland. Without such a centre, it is argued, the region will remain as two economic systems, whereas a commercial focus here could improve trade and promote international relations.

Preliminary studies have shown that German interest is greater than French because of the latter's doubts concerning their ability to invest in the German market. Initially the centre could concentrate on marketing French agricultural produce and a wholesale market, similar to that serving other major urban agglomerations, could be built. The project would involve co-operation in planning, of both the centre itself and the infrastructure to serve it.

The scheme has not, in fact, advanced since its proposal because it serves as a focus only for the eastern frontier region and because it was limited in its scope to supplementing the existing urban nuclei, Saarbrücken, Forbach, and Sarreguemines. However, the concept has been modified by the I.R.I. to that of a trans-frontier urban region, the planning of which is truly international. The I.R.I. report on a study conference which looked at a long-term structure for Saar/Lor/Lux envisages two trans-frontier agglomerations: (i) East Lorraine/Saarland, and (ii) South Luxembourg/North Lorraine. Both of these agglomerations could then be regarded as subregions in the plan of the larger structure, considered below.

Airports as regional foci
Two final examples of international efforts reveal both the potential for co-operation and the fact that national suspicion still looms large. It is obvious that a region of 4·8 million persons in 1985 will need a major airport and that such an airport can help to provide a focus to the region. If the airport is large and the service fast and frequent, then more industrialists may be attracted to the region. This is the argument for a regional airport to replace the four competing, local airports. At present Luxembourg possesses an international airport at Findel, but its traffic is small. The airport is close to the city but it creates problems of noise for the inhabitants of the southern suburbs. All the other airports (at Ensheim in Saarland, Nancy-Essey, and Metz-Frescaty) concentrate on internal flights with tourist charters in the summer season.

Since an airport is a status symbol for any region, the protagonists of trans-frontier co-operation would like to see one regional airport. To Luxembourg the downgrading of Findel airport could be regarded as the downgrading of

her status. To the Saarland, having just invested heavily in Ensheim, a regional airport could mean a misinvestment. Thus the Saarland prefers to see Ensheim as a potential regional airport, although runway expansion would be most expensive. The French also have a potential airport in Lorraine, half-way between Metz and Nancy at Louvigny, which could replace the two city airports. Faced with all this national rivalry, those in favour of co-operation have promoted the former military airfield at Grostenquin close to the Metz-Saarbrücken motorway and in a relatively sparsely peopled area of East Lorraine. The airport would have easy road communications to two of the agglomerations of the region. For the time being, however, national and subregional pride has won, and Saar/Lor/Lux will not have a major airport which would have attracted international flights.

Recreation
By contrast, schemes involving the delimitation of recreational zones and the siting of water-supply reservoirs have been much more successful. In 1964, six years before the Council of Europe adopted its recommendation on the creation of regional and trans-frontier natural parks, Rheinland-Pfalz and the Duchy of Luxembourg signed a treaty which established the Deutsch-Luxemburgischer Naturpark covering 740 km² in the Our and Sauer valleys north of Echternach to the Belgian frontier, having as its aim the preservation of natural beauty and recreation. This scheme also involved cross-frontier bridges. In the same area, an agreement has been reached for Luxembourg to receive water from the Prum and Bitburg areas of Pfalz.

There is a further, dual recreation and water-supply scheme on the Franco-German frontier to the south-west of Saarlouis. Here, in the Bisten-Horten area, an artificial reservoir is to be constructed to supply Saarlouis with water, at the same time providing a zone for aquatic sports.

Political initiatives
Over the last ten years the number of official and semi-official groups that have shown an interest in the region and its problems has grown very rapidly as the problems have made themselves manifest. The earliest organization to stimulate trans-frontier co-operation was the Commission d'Etudes Interrégionales Semois-Moselle-Sarre. The Conference for Regional Planning in North-West Europe began a study of the area in 1970 although it had been interested in frontier areas for over a decade. The stock exchanges in Nancy,

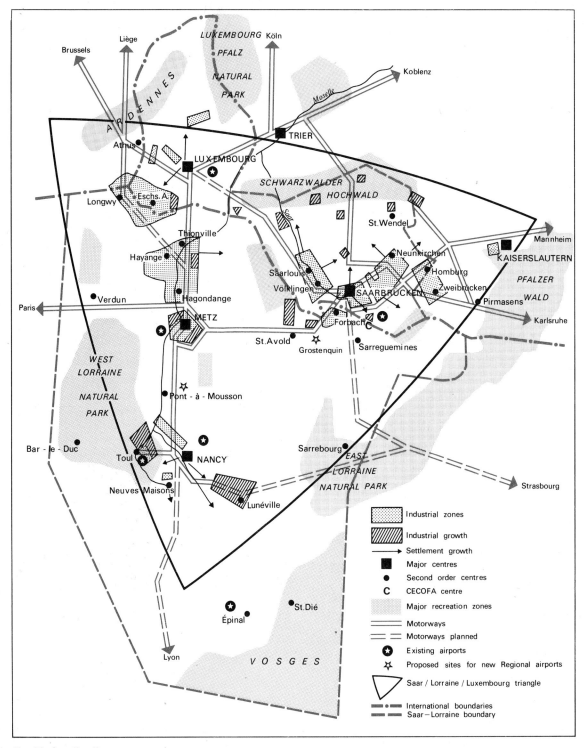

Fig. 10. Saar/Lor/Lux structure plans

Liège
Köln
LUXEMBOURG
PFALZ
Brussels
NATURAL
PARK
Moselle
Koblenz
TRIER
Athus
LUXEMBOURG
SCHWARZWALDER
HOCHWALD
Longwy
Eschs. A.
St.Wendel
Mannheim
Thionville
Neunkirchen
KAISERSLAUTERN
Hayange
Saarlouis
Homburg
PFALZER
Völklingen
SAARBRÜCKEN
Zweibrücken
WALD
Paris
Verdun
Hagondange
C
Pirmasens
METZ
St.Avold
Forbach
Karlsruhe
Grostenquin
Sarreguemines
WEST
LORRAINE
Pont - à - Mousson
NATURAL
PARK
Sarrebourg
EAST
Bar - le - Duc
Toul
LORRAINE
NATURAL PARK
Strasbourg
NANCY
Neuves Maisons
Lunéville
St.Dié
Épinal
Lyon
V O S G E S

	Industrial zones
	Industrial growth
→	Settlement growth
■	Major centres
●	Second order centres
C	CECOFA centre
	Major recreation zones
	Motorways
	Motorways planned
✪	Existing airports
✿	Proposed sites for new Regional airports
◁	Saar / Lorraine / Luxembourg triangle
	International boundaries
	Saar—Lorraine boundary

42

Luxembourg, Trier, and Saarbrücken have been co-operating in financing industrial investment in the region. In 1969 a Saar/Lor/Lux parliamentary commission was established to discuss regional development problems at annual meetings. In the following year a Franco-German regional commission for frontier co-operation was established, and in 1971 a similar link was developed between West Germany and Luxembourg. Frontier co-operation had been officially recognized and was rationalized in 1971 with the creation of the Saar/Lor/Lux Regional Commission.

The Regional Commission usually meets twice a year and has set up several study groups. The Bisten-Horten recreational zone was the subject of the earliest study, and this led to the establishment of a much more significant Regional Planning Group. Other groups are examining transport problems, the supply of water and waste disposal, and labour migration; in addition, but only since 1974, there is a statistical study group.

On the whole the Commission is making progress, but progress is slow because of differences in the political systems. Until recently the more centralized French system has meant that decisions had to be approved in Paris, whereas, under the German federal system, decision-making has often been located in Saarbrücken. Little has been done to reduce the psychological tensions of the region. The migrations of people and capital and the fluctuating monetary systems all raise suspicion, and the result is that 'there seems to be no limit to the fantasy of officials in devising difficulties to local co-operation across frontiers' (Strassoldo 1973). There can be difficulties in finding the appropriate opposite number when governmental systems vary. Because the Commission has no executive powers, it can only discuss issues, being full of goodwill but without the ability to turn that goodwill into the realities of international co-operation.

Regional planning structures

Although the States of the Saar/Lor/Lux triangle might find it difficult to indicate more than a handful of successes, they are able to point to good intentions embodied in the structure plans for the region. Whilst these plans might give every appearance of being prepared either for the *Land* or province, they do at least recognize the broader region (Fig. 10).

The 1971 *Raumordnungsbericht* for Rheinland-Pfalz acknowledges the need for trans-frontier co-operation in the field of regional planning since the *Land* borders France, Luxembourg, and Belgium by including a section on international co-operation. The Pfalzerwald Naturpark, which was established in 1958, provided a broad buffer zone of 1793 km² to the east of the region. However, the plan does not attempt to incorporate more than work that is already in progress in the Regional Commission.

The *Strukturprogramm* for the Saarland (1970) also sees the *Land* within the broader regional context, both in terms of the regional action programme and in terms of it being a constituent part of the trans-frontier, coalfield, industrial region and the Saar/Lor/Lux industrial triangle. There is a conscious effort to integrate planning strategies with those of the broader region and Western Europe, but some of the schemes suggest that the Saarland's interests are paramount. For example, the emphasis on the motorway extension towards Paris and the idea of a Seine–Saar–Rhine canal could be seen as efforts to use international schemes to improve the region's centrality.

The V-shaped Saar industrial region extending from Dillingen in the west to Neunkirchen and Homburg in the east is seen as the focus of industrial activity, although much of the growth in settlement is foreseen at each extremity of the V and beyond. The greatest suburban development will take place in the smaller towns such as Merzig, Blieskastel, Lebach, and St. Wendel, which had already become desirable commuter settlements in the 1960s. The north of the Saarland is a recreational zone, with several centres in the 680-km² Schwarzwalder Hochwald, such as Weiskirchen and Nonnweiler, being selected as growth points for tourism and weekend recreational activity.

The recreational zones of the Schwarzwalder Hochwald and the Deutsch-Luxemburgischer Naturpark were seen by an I.R.I. conference as part of a northern recreational fringe to the region, acting as a distinct break from surrounding regions to the north. It was also felt that the links between the Saarland and West Pfalz were not very strong because West Pfalz still looked eastwards to Mannheim. Similarly, the links between Saarbrücken and East Lorraine were noted but comments brought out the lack of strong integration.

In Lorraine much of the regional planning activity has been focused on the *métropole d'équilibre* Metz/Nancy/Thionville which is seen as the growth area for both industry and settlement, there being more space in this area than in the more crowded Saarland. The axis is seen as extending into southern Luxembourg to give the extended urban region an I shape, the base stretching from Toul to Lunéville and the top from Longwy to Luxembourg. It is anticipated that this region will continue to attract jobs and cater for the growth in population.

Outside the Moselle axis the other main zone of economic activity will continue to be East Lorraine although it is not seen as a major growth zone, but rather an urban area undergoing conversion. From the French point of view this area is already regarded as economically integrated with the Saarbrücken area, owing to the massive labour movements across the boundary. Some growth is anticipated in the other urban areas (Verdun, Bar-le-Duc, Epinal, and St. Dié), but this will be small if projections of current trends are accurate.

Beyond the urban growth areas, the overlap with German and Luxembourg strategies for recreational planning becomes apparent. The Parc Naturel Régional de Lorraine was established following extensive discussions. This Regional Park covers 169 000 hectares in two large sections. The larger portion is in the west, extending in a quadrilateral from Metz almost to Verdun, south to Toul, and east to Pont-à-Mousson. The smaller section is east of Nancy in the plateau area and includes many lakes with their wide variety of water birds. The park is seen as part of a green zone, skirting the Lorraine growth pole with its two million inhabitants who will constitute the major users of the park. On a wider scale these two parks are part of a ring of such recreational areas located around the Saar/Lor/Lux triangle and including Schwarzwalder Hochwald, Luxembourg Ardennes, Belgian Ardennes, the Lorraine parks, and the Pfalzerwald and Haguenau forest in the extreme east.

Lorraine also includes, in its south-east corner, part of the more important recreational region of the Vosges. Plans anticipate the continuing concentration of tourism in centres such as Longemer and Gérardmer, and the growth of skiing at high-altitude resorts such as La Schlucht, although most of these lack the range of entertainment of centres like Gérardmer. The Vosges also contain a handful of spas which are small and relatively unknown outside France. Plombières, Bains-les-Bains, and, just beyond the Vosges, Vittel are small tourist centres as well as spas.

It is generally felt that the above strategy which concentrates on the Lorraine *métropole d'équilibre* serves to unite the whole of Lorraine, and the extension of the *métropole* northwards to Luxembourg provides a strategy for international co-operation with Luxembourg, but not with the Saarland. The strategy for the *métropole* also neglects many of the more peripheral areas such as western Meuse and Vosges which are not drawn into international planning.

In the Duchy of Luxembourg industrial growth is to be kept to the southern half of the country whilst, at the same time, preventing an overconcentration in the Luxembourg/Esch-sur-Alzette sector. There are four zones chosen for industrial expansion: (i) east of Esch-sur-Alzette, (ii) the Ettelbrück-Diekirch area in the centre of the Duchy, (iii) west of Luxembourg, and (iv) around Steinfort. In broad terms the Luxembourg strategy reconfirms the threefold division of the Duchy into: (i) the sparsely populated north dominated by agriculture and an increasingly important tourist industry; (ii) the centre/east where agriculture, tourism, and viticulture in the Moselle valley, coexist with small industrial centres; and (iii) the centre-south dominated by industry and the service employment of Luxembourg City.

Looking at the plans that have been formulated in all three countries, there is a suggestion of a future region based on two major agglomerations, Luxembourg/Moselle and Saarland/East Lorraine, with a green heart separating them. Some even see similarities with the Dutch Randstad, although, as in the Netherlands, the ring is open to the east and a 'wing' concept is more appropriate. Beyond the urban core is the recreational fringe (Fig. 10).

At a conference organized by the I.R.I., the participants were asked to summarize the advantages and disadvantages of planning for the whole region, and to assess the degree of integration that already existed between the major political subregions. It was felt that a common approach to planning would raise three minor European regions to the status of one major centre of development in the E.E.C. and give the overall region greater dynamism. It would benefit from the increased scale of activities and would attract better facilities for the population if it were treated as a whole rather than as three parts. Overall strategies would serve to reduce competition between the three States. Plans for recreation needed immediate harmonization because, as we have seen, weekend tourists know no boundaries, and the Germans spend weekends in France and the French spend weekends in Luxembourg. It was felt that planning at the international level could create areas of activity

Lac de Longemer, Vosges. A recreational area in the Vosges mountains and part of the girdle of recreational zones surrounding the Saar/Lor/Lux triangle

which would produce higher per capita incomes, optimum industrial conditions, and higher productivity. International planning would also achieve improved status for the region *vis-à-vis* the successful regions of the Community such as Rhein/Main and the Lower Rhône valley.

On the other hand, the delegates also drew attention to several disadvantages of an international approach to regional planning. There is a danger that an international approach would not be democratic because the democratic procedures necessary for such a planning venture do not exist. To improve the dynamism of this region could result in the slowing down of regional growth elsewhere in the four States, or it could make other regions still more peripheral to the major growth zones. The delegates were worried that the growth of Saar/Lor/Lux might retard the growth of Alsace or Schleswig-Holstein for example, or make more acute the problems of periphery of Brittany or south-east Bavaria. Perhaps the most important constraint was the fact that an international approach to planning in this region would raise economic, judicial, and social constraints, which would be necessary for the success of regional planning, but which would result in a reduction in the freedom of individual States and, perhaps, their sovereignty. However, some alignment by the nations making up the region will be necessary if any progress is to be made in solving the regional planning problems. Some go as far as to suggest that if solutions cannot be found in such border regions of the E.E.C. as Saar/Lor/Lux, then the future for European union will remain bleak.

The delegates outlined certain preconditions for successful trans-frontier planning. They felt, for example, that there needed to be a basis in international law for such planning. Regional proposals ought to be worked out by collaboration rather than in isolation, and the agreed proposals should be translated into reality using a regional development fund that could finance plans throughout the region. Since everything proposed could not be achieved at once, a list of priorities needed to be agreed for the different levels of planning. Finally, the delegates saw the now-completed regional reforms in France, and local government re-organization in Germany as potential threats to international co-operation because they could create administrative arrangements that would impede future collaboration.

45

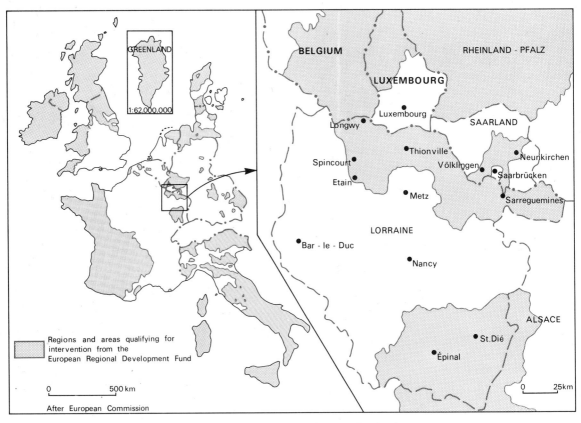

Fig. 11. European Commission zones qualifying for Regional Development Fund aid

European Community solutions

The idea of a region based on two agglomerations with their surrounding expanding residential areas and peripheral open spaces, giving the region a green envelope and a green heart, was supported. Infrastructural improvements were envisaged such as rapid transit rail links (e.g. METROLOR) extended to cross the boundaries, an international network of pipelines to carry oil products, and a single regional airport. The delegates were also conscious of the water needs and the problems of waste disposal and pollution posed by a major urban industrial region at the heart of Europe. It was also recommended that in the field of education syllabuses be synchronized, bilingualism encouraged, and foreign qualifications recognized. All these proposals would encourage mobility and reduce the psychological factor that many regard as the stumbling block to greater co-operation.

European Community solutions
The problems of Saar-Lorraine, whether they arise from peripheral location within the respective States, the presence of a boundary, or the structural problems of the region, have been approached at both the local and the regional/international level. Some solutions have been proposed and the success of these, as we have seen, will depend on international co-operation. But because the problems of this region cannot be tackled in the isolated context of Saar-Lorraine without affecting other areas, the problem of frontier regions has become a European problem.

As long ago as 1963 the E.E.C. prepared a report on the Lorraine-Luxembourg region and the Meuse axis, but little resulted from the study. The European Coal and Steel Community also studied the structural problems of the region in the 1960s. In October 1973 the European Commission decided to set up a Regional Development Fund, and proposals for the operation of this fund have been made. The proposals, together with the delimitation of other problem regions by the Community, sets the Saar-Lorraine area in a wider perspective, relating the region's needs to those of other regions which might be affected by overgrowth or over-investment in this small part of the Community. The criteria for delimiting problem regions are: a lower gross domestic product than the Community average, heavy dependence on agricultural employment, heavy dependence on employment in declining industries, persistently high rates of unemployment, and a high rate of net emigration over a long period. It is anticipated that the grants will be made mainly to the more populated areas and not to isolated pockets with particular problems. The funds will also complement existing national regional policies.

The areas of Saar/Lor/Lux that have been designated as problem regions are not as extensive as the national definitions (Fig. 11). This is particularly the case in the Saarland where only two *Landkreise*, Ottweiler and Saarbrücken Land, have been included. However, neighbouring *Kreise* in Rheinland-Pfalz abutting on the northern Saarland, such as Trier-Saarburg and Bitburg-Prum, are regions qualifying for intervention from the development fund. Much of the north of Luxembourg also qualifies, as does the Belgian province of Luxembourg. Within Lorraine there are two zones qualifying for intervention. The first is the northern frontier zone including the ironfield, parts of northern Meuse (around Etain), Thionville, and the East Lorraine coalfield, Sarreguemines, and the Pays de Bitche. The second zone is the area around Epinal and St. Dié which is part of a broader Vosges mountain problem region.

The major cities of the region have been excluded from the definition because solutions to their problems have been advanced in national policies in the past two decades. The Commission's emphasis is on rural areas with problems, and on the structural problems resulting from the rationalization of mining and the iron and steel industry that were examined in Chapter Two. These problems are not peculiar to the Saar-Lorraine frontier region. Thus it could be argued that the criteria selected for delimiting the problem regions do not enable frontier regions to be seen as problem regions in their own right.

Council of Europe proposals

The Council of Europe, through its conference responsible for regional planning and its committee on co-operation in municipal and regional matters, has done much to publicize the problem of frontier regions. Commenting on a Franco-Belgian and Luxembourg region, one report states, 'Certain experiments have been undertaken in the Lorraine/Luxembourg region, but they have produced no tangible results.' In the case of Saar/Lorraine/Luxembourg the report refers to the tradition of contact over the past decade and tabulates such contacts.

A background paper, prepared by Strassoldo (1973) for the ministers responsible for regional planning, attempts to put forward solutions to the problems of frontier regions. These are proposals for all the frontier regions and not just Saar-Lorraine. However, they do form a fitting conclusion to this study. Strassoldo suggests that the Europeans should attempt to promote a series of psychological and cultural attitudes to trans-frontier co-operation. This could be done by promoting European values, by developing the concept of sociological regions that transcend boundaries, and by harnessing the forces of regional awareness that are stronger in frontier regions. Then, he suggests, trans-frontier awareness will emerge. Schools and the media can draw attention to the frontier region, as has happened in Saar-Lorraine with the simultaneous publication of supplements by the press.

Much emphasis is placed on smoothing the legal path to co-operation at all levels—international, national, and local. Institutions designed to cater for frontier regions, including Commissions like the one operating already in Saar-Lorraine, ought to be set up by the States. Regional planning of frontier zones (including the development of a methodology for the scientific definition of boundaries) is seen as a further key to lessening the impact of the boundary lines. Many planning proposals must be brought to fruition by consensus, although others will need institutions to back them up.

Conclusion

It is the 'territorial taboo' that Strassoldo sees as a major stumbling block. Nation States are reluctant to surrender their political and legal rights, expecially in frontier regions such as Saar-Lorraine, where the boundary has fluctuated so much and with so many terrifying consequences. This problem can be overcome only by the creation of supra-national authorities for co-operation in a region (or regions) that slowly erode sovereignty whilst promoting regional consciousness. Progress will be slow because suspicions linger on, but one must hope that in Saar-Lorraine the legacy of yesterday, expressed in terms of frontier location and a variety of economic problems, becomes a basis for progress in the unified Europe of tomorrow.

Further Work

Reading

Because many works of the past have concerned themselves with the national units, the further reading is inevitably broad in scope. I. B. Thompson, *Modern France: A Social and Economic Geography* (Batsford, 1972) gives a valuable introduction to Lorraine and its regional planning structure and industrial decentralization. D. Burtenshaw, *An Economic Geography of West Germany* (Macmillan, 1974) introduces the problems of energy and the iron and steel industry in a national context, besides outlining regional planning problems. R. C. Riley and G. J. Ashworth, *Benelux* (Chatto and Windus, 1974) deals with relevant themes such as regional planning and industrial development in Luxembourg.

The major sources of material used in the text are reports prepared by the various regional organizations and international bodies. The Council of Europe has published a series of articles on frontier regions of which R. Strassoldo's 'Frontier Regions and Regional Planning', CEMAT (73) BP10 (Council of Europe, Strasbourg, 1973) and V. F. von Malchus 'The Cooperation of European Frontier Regions', AS/COLL. Front (72)1 (Council of Europe, Strasbourg, 1972) are the most useful.

Other readily accessible references used in the preparation of the text were:

CLOUT, H. D., 'French Population Growth 1962–8', *Geography* **56**, 2 (1971).

MARTIN, J. E., 'Industrial Employment and Investment in a Frontier Region: The Franco-German Example', *Geography* **58**, 1 (1973).

MARTIN, J. E., 'Some Effects of the Canalization of the Moselle,' *Geography* **59**, 4 (1974).

SCARGILL, D. I., 'Energy in France', *Geography* **58**, 2 (1973).

The locally-produced geographical journals, *Mosella* in particular, *Annals de L'Est*, and *Saarbrücker Geographische Arbeiten* contain articles on the region. The monthly, *Actualités Industrielle Lorraines*, is a most valuable source of information on the iron and steel industry. *Les Dossiers de L'Economie de Lorraine* published by I.N.S.E.E. at Nancy has many articles on the economy and demography. The occasional reports from the Institut für regionalpolitische Zusammenarbeit in innergeinschaftlichen Grenz-raumen (I.R.I.) in Saarbrücken provide a unique international perspective on the region's difficulties. The statistical sources used were furnished by the Statistisches Landesamt in Saarbrücken, S.T.A.T.E.C. in Luxembourg and I.N.S.E.E. in Nancy. Statistics from companies and industrial associations have also been used.

Maps and atlases

There are three excellent atlases covering the region. *Deutsche Planungsatlas*, Band X *Saarland* (Hannover, 1965) has a comprehensive set of maps although it is becoming dated. The *Atlas d l'Est* (Nancy, 1969) has been revised recently. The *Atlas de Luxembourg* (Luxembourg, 1971) also contains a wealth of information. The French 1:100 000 and the German 1:50 000 series can be used although the settlement, communication patterns and economic information are dated.

The Regional Economic Atlas of Western Europe (O.U.P., 1973) provides useful background information relating to the whole region.

Comparative study

Problem frontier regions abound in the European Economic Community. While no others have the problem of a fluctuating boundary, there are many areas where similar economic problems exist on either side of the boundary. Reference to H. D. Clout, *The Franco-Belgian Border Region,* and W. R. Mead, *The Scandinavian Northlands*, in the Problem Regions of Europe series would provide contrasts with Saar-Lorraine. R. Strassoldo's article on frontier regions mentioned above provides the most up-to-date catalogue of all the frontier commissions and agreements. The economic problems of the region can also be compared with those elaborated by J. A. Hellen for *North Rhine-Westphalia* and K. Warren for *North East England* in the Problem Regions of Europe series.